PILGRIMAGE
IN
MISSION

DONALD R. JACOBS

FOREWORD BY
WILBERT R. SHENK

Wipf & Stock
PUBLISHERS
Eugene, Oregon

Wipf and Stock Publishers
199 W 8th Ave, Suite 3
Eugene, OR 97401

Pilgrimage in Mission
By Jacobs, Donald R.
Copyright©1983 Herald Press
ISBN 13: 978-1-55635-277-5
ISBN 10: 1-55635-277-8
Publication date: 2/16/2007
Previously published by Herald Press, 1983

To Anna Ruth Jacobs,
a tireless, sensitive wife, mother,
and Christian sister
whose inspiration finds expression
in this book.

CONTENTS

FOREWORD

A search is on to find new word-pictures to describe Christian mission. Words of course are but symbols and symbols have a way of losing their power over us. In that respect words are like fashions which are constantly being renewed because the times in which we live change and people's tastes change.

Pilgrimage in Mission is a pledge that the search is indeed worthwhile. It firmly grasps the foundation of mission in Jesus Christ, on the one hand, while exploring what missionary faithfulness requires in the coming decades on the other.

We must conduct this search amid disintegration in the world. The West has in the space of several centuries traversed to the heights of political and economic power, only to plummet into a period of crisis. Politically, the world is under increasing stress. The old political order cannot cope with a vastly changed world. Multinational corporations exert more influence on the world economy, and therefore on international relations, than a majority of the nation states which make up the United Nations organization. The destructive forces in the world seem to outweigh the constructive ones.

Such a sense of disintegration arises out of the transition from one era to another. What was known as Christendom dominated world affairs since the Middle Ages. Christendom exists no more. The way people looked at the world in the nineteenth and early twentieth centuries appears increasingly quaint to us as we approach the twenty-first century.

We smile today at the audacity of missionary leaders who at the turn of the twentieth century placarded the slogan, "The Evangelization of the World in This Generation," before student conventions and church audiences. It so obviously fit its times but hardly suits us today. It became a potent tool at the time for rallying missionary recruits and support because it effectively summed up the mood and expectations of the day: the West would inevitably be world leader. Christian ideals and values commended themselves to the rest of the world. The challenge was primarily that of proper strategy, organization, and promotion. But the triumphalism of Christendom rubbed raw the nerves of young leaders in Asia, Africa, and Latin America.

World War I shattered these pretensions to world domination by Christendom. Humpty Dumpty had taken his fateful fall, and Humpty Dumpty turned out to be the Western powers. The church in the West was closely tied to that collapse of Western influence.

A close reading of the Bible shows that a fresh mission thrust always begins in times of crisis—in the world and within God's people. In the Old Testament these new beginnings occurred when the people of Israel found themselves as exiles in strange lands among strange peoples. They found their mission when they were bereft of all political, economic, and historical security. At that moment they returned to true worship of the Lord Jehovah. Only then could he entrust them with the task of being his messengers to the world. It was when they "had no abiding city" that they found themselves emboldened to witness. In their moment of distress, they became strangely aware of the world which did not yet worship the God of Israel.

Donald R. Jacobs knows firsthand the exhilaration of being a pilgrim. His years in East Africa are an important backdrop to what he writes. The churches of East Africa have tasted bitter suffering as well as the gracious renewal of the Holy Spirit. A part of that reviving, renewing work of the Spirit touched such sensitive matters as the relations between blacks and whites, missionary and local church. Like ancient Israel, the church in Africa and elsewhere in the world must discover in each generation that in the cross of Jesus Christ we encounter God's saving power. But we also rediscover in the cross that God accepts all his children regardless of their particular culture. All cultures are equal in God's sight; all stand under the curse of sin. This fact calls all who are concerned for cross-cultural communication to start with a proper humility and respect for other peoples. Western cultural superiority ought to be the first casualty of the cross.

Pilgrimage in Mission exudes a biblically based optimism and enthusiasm about the future of mission. It calls us more fully to place our trust in the work and mission of Jesus. The crisis of our day is not the last word. To be sure, we need to take it seriously and seek to understand it, but we must do so in light of the gospel promise, "Behold, I am making all things new." God continues calling his people to be in diaspora for his sake and for the sake of the world.

As we dare to follow him, we will be truly pilgrims in mission. And that is a promising word-picture to help us understand mission for the next decades.

—Wilbert R. Shenk
Elkhart, Indiana

Lent 1983

WHY ANOTHER THEOLOGY OF MISSION?

This World, Friend or Foe?

Sunsets overwhelm me. One day while I was passing through a Somali desert the sun danced on the horizon. The sky lit up with an intensity I had never seen. I stood spellbound, flooded with a profound feeling of well-being: this world is astonishingly beautiful. I get this same impression when I see people caring for their aged and their handicapped. I am amazed how people love one another and how they do the unexpected whether they get credit or not. This world is a friendly, warm place. It is good to be here. I want to belong to this world. Nothing happens here which does not, to some extent, affect me. So, world, count me in.

That is one side of the picture. There is another side. When we are bathed in the warm glow of joy because of the beauty of it all, someone throws a bucket of cold water over our heads. We think of this world spending a million dollars a second perfecting its ability to slaughter one another. We see a self-centered value system shattering a third of American marriages. We see our young American women legally aborting more than a million of their pregnancies a year. Is this the world I am feeling so good about belonging to? Obviously not. World, count me out.

Do you identify with me? Do you, too, feel a strangeness about being here? The world is so beautiful, yet it is so disconcerting. How does one solve this problem? How did Jesus, the Creator of it all, solve it?

Go with me to the upper room. Jesus is sharing his vision with the disciples just hours before his crucifixion. He put his thoughts into a prayer. He prayed, "[Father,] I do not pray that thou shouldst take them out of the world, but that thou shouldst keep them from the evil one [in the world]" (John 17:15). In, but kept, that was the way Jesus put it.

Earlier on he sent out seventy evangelists two by two. He startled them with a rather humorous word picture. "Behold," he said, "I send you out as sheep in the midst of wolves" (Matthew 10:16). The evangelists were like sheep sent to the wolves. Our first impression is, poor sheep because wolves have sheep for dinner, literally. Talk about a dilemma! Have things changed today? Have we become the wolves and the world the sheep? Hardly. We are frighteningly vulnerable.

"The Christian life is not difficult," I heard someone say recently. "It is impossible." That is putting it rather bluntly but it does at least highlight the problem. If we understand Jesus correctly, he told his disciples to be "in" the world as citizens of nations, eaters of earth's foods, and speakers of human languages; yet, and here is where the rub comes, not to be "of" the world, that is, not to be the world's children.

All believers sense that they are, in a sense, aliens, foreigners. They are not fully comfortable in the world.

They feel a tension between their new life in Christ and the world around them which has no place for him. Jesus put his finger squarely on the issue when, in that same upper room, he continued his prayer, reporting to God, "As thou didst send me into the world, so I have sent them into the world" (John 17:18). Explaining the "so," he said further, "The world has hated them because they are not of the world, even as I am not of the world" (John 17:14b). And if Jesus lives in his followers, they will be in trouble just like he was. It boils down to that. As one of our hymns puts it, "This world is not a friend to grace."

Christians are in trouble, constant trouble, because of the very nature of the gospel itself and the nature of this "world." They are not responsible for the dilemma, they did not create it, they were reborn into it! Everything a follower of Jesus does is immediately and ultimately affected by the enmity which is created when some creatures say "yes" to Jesus and others say "no" to him. Do you have the feeling of being alienated by the world? I expect you have if you are at all sincere about living Christ's life on earth. You face this alienation every morning. It sets the stage on which your life is acted out.

This world is in reality two worlds: one of them resists Jesus Christ and the other receives and follows him. We are all born into that first world, no matter if dad is a bishop and mom a deaconess, or if one's parents never heard of Jesus. The way to get transferred from one to the other is through a transformation. Jesus calls it being born again. We all affirm that. It is in the Bible. But the tougher question comes, "What should be our relationship to the world which we left?" Furthermore, is Jesus completely absent from that world we left? How different should we be from that world?

Or the question can be put as a missionary question,

"What does a missionary (or an evangelist) call people to and what are they called out of? What, ultimately, is the relationship between these two opposing kingdoms? Is the kingdom of God a visible, separate community, or does it 'lose' itself in identification with those who have not yet believed?"

Admittedly, the goal of missions is to assist as many people as possible to move from the kingdom which resists Jesus to the kingdom in which he is loved and is acknowledged as Savior and Lord. But how do we understand that process? What is our theology and our understanding of the sociology of mission? How does it work?

Anyone who knows anything at all about the Anabaptist-Mennonite tradition knows that this series of questions has dominated their inner life for many decades. But every denomination which has any history at all finds itself in the same quandary. The history of every denomination, and the Mennonite church in particular, is a fascinating tale of how they tried and are trying to solve the tension between the "pro-in-the world" and the "anti-world" factions of the church.

We now arrive at the purpose of this book. It is to study what part modern missions have played in increasing and decreasing these tensions within the brotherhood; to propose a way of understanding missions whose foundation is scriptural; and to reflect on some of the lessons God has taught us Anabaptist Mennonites who have been preserved and nurtured for over 450 years by God. Underlying this purpose is the premise that God's most profound desire is that all people everywhere would come to Jesus and find in him their Savior and their Lord and would then form communities which are enthused by divine love. It is only in participating with God in his mission that the Anabaptist people and, for that matter, any denomination, find fulfillment. So this study is not only a study of the church's mission but of the church itself.

The Shaken Mennonites

The Anabaptists upset a heap of applecarts in their first two decades (1525 to 1545). As people were converted they were rebaptized, much to the chagrin of the Catholics who had made a big point of authenticating their sacrament of baptism. Refusing to take up arms to defend any state, whether Catholic or Reformed, they got into trouble with both sides. By insisting that they could not take an oath, they were marked as highly unpredictable people, an unacceptable state of affairs as far as governments and courts were concerned. A host of other problems surfaced and the Anabaptists were effectively quarantined by their respective governments in much the same way people with measles are quarantined.

Having rejected much Catholic teaching of the time, they were in turn rejected. What followed was an era of relative isolation. The Anabaptist-Mennonite communities saw themselves as marginal people. They, therefore, began to slowly spin for themselves a Germanic cultural cocoon which served them well for over 350 years. They took this cocoon with them everywhere they migrated in the world. Their culture and their religious life were very much one and the same. During this period their medium of thought and communication was German or Dutch. At the turn of the last century it was rare indeed to find a Mennonite anywhere in the world (except for the few in Indonesia) who could not speak German or Dutch. In fact, in 1900 almost all Mennonite worship was conducted in the German or Dutch languages even though the congregations were scattered beyond Germany and Holland to the United States, Canada, and Russia. Because it was a rather closed socio-religious community, the denomination depended upon their own children to perpetuate the church rather than adding members through aggressive evangelism. The result was that cultural identity was assured. It was like that for 375 years.

Then, about the turn of the century, Mennonites began to be rather aggressive in evangelizing non-Germanic people at home and abroad. They incorporated these non-Germanic people into their fellowships or started new fellowships. The result of this evangelistic vigor is a truly multi-cultural brotherhood, a universal church. Today Mennonites speak a multitude of languages. They conduct their religious services in at least fifty-six languages, a sociological seismograph of a colossal social upheaval: German, Dutch, Russian, Spanish, English, French, Luxembourgish, Italian, Javanese, Amharic, Ga, Krobe, Shai, Luo, Efik, Ndebele, Somali, Swahili, Kutuba, Lingala, Tshiluba, Tonga, Hindi, Bengali, Telugu, Indonesian, Japanese, Togalog, Taiwanese, Mandarin, Portuguese, Trique, Kekchi, Cheyenne, Hopi, Kijita, Kikuria, Cantonese, Vietnamese, Hebrew, Garifuna, Korean, Lengua, Chulipi, Sarapona, Guarani, Haitian Creole, Quichua, American Sioux, Gipende, Chokwe, Toba, Laotian, Cree, Saulteaux, Sign, and maybe a few more. Most Mennonites, however, now speak English and only a handful use German in ordinary conversation. This is one reason why we describe the change of the past eight decades as a "shaking."

As long as Mennonites did not evangelize and fellowship with people of other cultures, they proceeded undisturbed, enjoying their "Germanic" life wherever they established their communities, whether in the Russian Ukraine, in

English Philadelphia, or elsewhere. So even though the vast majority of the Mennonites lived outside of Germanic Europe by 1900, they were German nevertheless, especially in their most deeply-held religious views. Outsiders got the impression that you had to be "born" a Mennonite to become one, a view not unheard of even today. The result was that walls grew up around the Mennonite communities, walls built with both cultural and religious bricks. One of the ways they tested the faithfulness of new believers was to find out how serious they were about joining Germanic-Mennonite culture. During this period, if a member in North America was backsliding he was "becoming English," it was said. So closely was cultural identity tied to religious faithfulness. The Amish, a Mennonite branch, still require strict adherence to a code of behavior fashioned in their Germanic societies.

It is little wonder, therefore, that Mennonite theology from 1560 to 1900 concentrated on the "not of this world" part of the gospel because they were, indeed, not like their neighbors. Their cultural uniqueness created distance between themselves and their neighbors. Nowhere was this as dramatic as in Russia where the Mennonites were given certain privileges denied to native Russian Christians on the understanding that they would not evangelize Russians. During those years the Mennonites concentrated on nurturing their children. And, to be fair to them, they could have hardly afforded the luxury of losing their cultural identity or they would have been assimilated into Russian life and thereby have lost their prophetic stance, their very reason for existence. Mennonites viewed themselves as different and society returned the favor.

It was almost without warning, then, that less than fifty years ago large segments of the Mennonites (not in Russia, however, where a Mennonite split occurred over this and other issues) opened their doors to non-Germanic people. Humpty-Dumpty fell off the wall and the homogeneous past was gone forever; or to use another metaphor, the cocoon was so badly split open that it could never be reentered again. This was especially true of the Mennonite churches in North America.

"This would not have happened," some say rather nostalgically, "if the Mennonites had not jumped onto the modern evangelical bandwagon which insisted on mission." There is a lot of truth in that statement but it would be going too far to suggest that all of the tensions which disturbed the church in the past fifty years resulted from its involvement in cross-cultural missions. Many waves of influence swept across the Mennonite communities in North America during that period and they would have changed had they been in mission or not. Particularly important was the fact that Canada and the United States fought two wars against people who spoke German!

The church's newfound involvement in aggressive cross-cultural ministries did pose new theological questions. The theology of separation which they had developed so successfully in their separatistic communities was challenged by their theology of evangelism which insists that the gospel should be taken to all men everywhere. Had they abandoned their theology of separation, they would have compromised their convictions on maintaining a "pure church." On the other hand, to stop evangelizing both within and beyond one's own culture was equally unacceptable because the mission imperative is clearly biblical and they were, above all else, biblical.

But to keep in balance a theology of separation and a theology of evangelism is not an easy matter. In fact, the struggle between these two schools of thought became so intense that the unity of the brotherhood was threatened. The Mennonite dilemma is clear: "Does God want us to build a pure church or a missionary church?" This dilemma is still with us and it has a lot to do with how we feel about missions.

For Mennonites, hopefully this book can help update our understanding of how we can maintain both a vision for a "pure church" and a vision for a "missionary church." I assume we must do both if we are to be faithful disciples of Jesus Christ. I am convinced that there will always be tension between the two. I am also convinced that we can avoid being paralyzed by the tension if we fully comprehend the totality of the gospel of Jesus Christ.

We will begin this study by examining some modern theologies of mission or evangelism which I call "theologies of relevance." Then we will turn to an examination of the theologies of separation from the world which I call "theologies of confrontation." After surveying each school of thought we will scrutinize each in the light of New Testament and Anabaptist themes. Finally we will trace our own recent experience as a denomination. The result should be not only a better understanding of where we have come from but, even more importantly, where the Holy Spirit is leading us in the future. I intend to propose a theology which will take seriously both sides of the statement of Jesus that we are "in the world" but "not of the world."

I will speak from within the brotherhood, yet I speak out of personal search and experience. I acknowledge that I perceive, as it were, "through a glass darkly." I see only in part. Furthermore, I cannot speak for everybody.

I speak, also, as a participant. I do not stand outside of the action like a referee or an observer, but I am myself in the "game." I accept the fact that I am part of the theologizing process itself. I cannot speak for all Mennonites, but primarily for myself, a Christian in the Mennonite tradition who stands within a moment of history. I have been fashioned by the context of my own involvement in mission over the past years, first as a person to whom the gospel came, then as a communicator of that gospel as a missionary, and then as a mission board administrator.

Saying this, perhaps I can be forgiven for both my excesses and lack of total comprehension. Perhaps my many deficiencies will be compensated for in part by my intense involvement in the life and ministry of the worldwide brotherhood.

—Donald R. Jacobs
Landisville, Pennsylvania

NOTE: A separate booklet is available to facilitate the study of this material in group settings. Ask for *Pilgrimage in Mission Leader's Guide* by Richard A. Kauffman (Herald Press, 1983).

PILGRIMAGE
IN
MISSION

1

GOD MEETS MAN

Jesus Meets Human Need

Jacob had had a rough night. With a rock for a pillow and the wilderness sand for his mattress he tried to get some sleep. He was desperately needy, having just lied and stolen. Then he dreamt of that famous ladder with one end in the heavens and with the other end beside him. Angels were going up and down ministering to his needs. This was a new idea to him; God is concerned about his needs. He need not take things into his own hands; in fact, the best thing he can do is to pray and cooperate with God.

The whole Bible is really a great story about how God does everything in his power to make his abundance available to people right where they are. And missionaries in turn try the best they can to help people to open their lives to God who is very much concerned about meeting human need. Their success or lack of it does not take away from the fact that God wants to help people.

When I was teaching in a Tanzanian Bible school early in my missionary career, I attended a meeting of people just like myself, missionary teachers who had been trained in the West but now were struggling valiantly to teach something meaningful to their eager African students. In our more sober moments we had the uneasy feeling that what we taught was not really geared to African needs. But we were undaunted.

Then in this meeting a straightforward American brother openly admitted that he could not answer many of the students' questions, especially those dealing with demons, witchcraft, the curse, the nature of illness and blessing, and so forth, because he could not comprehend the African world. After this outburst of frustration, someone came up with a simple solution: "We must teach our students the right questions." He said it half jokingly, yet half seriously. I gather what he meant was, "We must teach them the questions for which we have nice, pat answers." At times our teaching was like smiling at someone in total darkness. We know what we are doing but the other person does not get much benefit from our effort.

How much, we might ask, is the gospel supposed to answer local questions? Why should we attempt to address the particular local needs of people? Are not everyone's needs, after all, the same everywhere in the world? Said in yet another way, How much should we shape the gospel to meet the needs of people who do not experience life like we do? What part does the missionary play in this process? Is this not the responsibility of the Holy Spirit?

The questions come to us fast and heavy when we attempt to put into practice Christ's commission to take the good news to every man. As long as we evangelize our own kind, the problem is not as severe: being culturally similar, "we understand one another." The picture gets very complicated, however, when we begin to evangelize and nurture others across cultural boundaries. Then we need guiding principles, a theology of relevance which takes local need seriously.

If all the nations of the world (its cultures, subcultures, clans) are to see in Christ the answers to their aspirations, then the gospel must be presented to each of these "nations" in such a way that Jesus Christ becomes relevant and real, that is, so that he is not just seen as a quaint or fascinating personality who lived long ago in some strange land but as a living presence who is eager to become active in one's own life and community.

Theologies that help this to happen take seriously Jesus' words that the church is "in" the world and must, therefore, actually be a part of that world. Jesus used two symbols to make this point, salt and light (Matthew 5). If salt and light are to do any good at all, they must reach their object; in fact, they must enter into the very substance of that which they are to influence. Salt and light must become relevant to that which they are to affect.

Separatistic or confrontationist theologies, on the other hand, concentrate on preserving the saltiness of the salt and the brightness of the light. (Jesus emphasized this aspect of the good news also.) The theologies of accommodation or relevance, the present topic of discussion, explore how to get the salt out of the shaker and on to the food or how light can get out to the world so that people will be able to live in its glory. What good is it, they contend, if the salt is salty but never gets involved with the world? Salt in a plastic bag deposited in a soup will not alter the taste of the soup. We might say the salt must "get with" the soup if it is to make any difference at all. And what good is a brightly burning lamp if you put it inside a safe?

It is easy to see that concentrating on holy separateness, keeping the salt salty, militates to some degree against evangelism. If evangelism is anything, it is making Jesus Christ available to meet people's needs. For this reason missionaries tend to major on developing theologies of accommodation while those who are responsible for the maintenance of nurture ministries in the church tend to major on the themes of separation and purity. And this is part of our problem. Somehow, we should get these two together. Each group needs the other.

God Reaches Out to Humankind

From Genesis 1 we read of God the Creator reaching out to one unique part of the entire creation, to human beings. He wants to mingle with people, to commune with them. He seems to be fascinated (and at times troubled) by humankind. He is very definitely for people. For this reason he appeared to them through prophets, the law, through visions, and through extraordinary interventions. He set a bush aflame to catch Moses' attention and divided the waters of the Red Sea to deliver his people. He clearly demonstrated in a thousand ways that he is driven with compassion to become available to people, to be relevant to their needs. It is as though he is always trying to get their attention, saying, "People, I am here. I care about you. I have more to give you than you have ever dreamed possible. Walk in my law and live."

The story line of the Bible is clear. God provided everything that people could possibly desire for happiness. But they pushed him out of their lives and enthroned themselves in the place designed only for God. That is essentially what we refer to as the fall. The consequences of the fall were so profound that it caused God untold suffering. People suffered, too, as they slowly lost touch with their Creator. Genesis describes this profound alienation in great detail and with utmost candor.

But the Creator God is also the redeeming God who always takes the initiative. He reaches down to bring humankind back into fellowship with himself, so that people can be recreated, or as Jesus described it at one point, "born again." People seek God, yet they reject him. Not so with God: he approaches people like a lover woos the beloved, as a shepherd gathers his sheep. Yet humankind spurns these efforts time and time again. They want it their way. But God never gives up. He doggedly seeks ways to bring people into harmony with himself, with their families, friends, neighbors, even their enemies, and finally into harmony with nature. But people fear God because they know that if God would do what he should do, he would destroy them. God's presence is fearsome. Even the disciples feared when Jesus stood among them after his resurrection. Jesus often said, "Be not afraid." In order to approach us, God must convince us that he is "on our side" and not against us. He is *for* people; he is relevant to their needs.

a. Creation—One Pillar for Missions

Theologies of accommodation are usually based upon the great themes of Creation. They proceed like this. God, the one who fashioned the race, knows assuredly what their needs are because he made them and, in addition, they share some part of his image. There is a direct link between God the Creator and humankind, the creature. "Let us make man in our image," is the witness of Scripture (Genesis 1:26.) No one knows what is in our hearts like the one who himself created us.

But we pushed God out of the picture, or at least tried to. We fell. It was not a case of simply ignoring God; we deliberately disobeyed the revealed will of God and by doing so we set ourselves against God which really placed us on the side of God's enemy, Satan.

As a result of the fall, Satan got control of some aspects of our world. What he controlled and how extensive that control was is not at all clear. But there is little doubt that after the fall Satan had a significant influence over those spirits which were in rebellion against God, including humanity. When Jesus speaks of the "world" (the age) which hates him (John 17:14), it is that "world" controlled by Satan which, also, is the world he instructed his disciples they were not to be "of."

The central teaching of creation and fall is that people must have intimate fellowship with God in order to be content, creative beings. As long as they persist in rejecting the truth so clearly expressed by God, they are destined to do damage to themselves and God's creation. St. Augustine said it well: "Man's heart is restless and finds no rest until it is at rest in God."

b. Incarnation, the Second Pillar for Missions

The second theological pillar upon which theologies of accommodation rest is the incarnation of Jesus. As the Old Testament closes, the drama heightens. When it appears as though God has exhausted all available methods to woo humankind back to himself, a child is born in Bethlehem who is none other than God himself. God came in human form in order to save us from our chronic tendency to try to "make it" on our own or to escape being human. This child was the Messiah, Jesus Christ, the supremely relevant one. The Word of God became flesh and dwelt among us (John 1:14).

He was named Emmanuel, "God with us." How more relevant can God get? Is it not almost as difficult for God to be
like us as it is for us to be like him? For him, incarnation was
terribly costly.

Theologies of accommodation see in the incarnation the
marvelous truth that God took the initiative to come down to
us so that a way could be opened for us to repent and to turn
to our Creator, now appearing in the flesh as Savior and
Lord. The incarnation not only brings salvation into our
experience, but it gives us a window into God's heart. Jesus,
God in the flesh, was always relevant because he met people
at their point of need and he walked with them into
freedom. He became like we are so that we could become
like he is (Hebrews 4:15).

When John the Baptist, in prison chains, sent messengers
to ask whether Jesus was the Messiah or if they should wait
for another, Jesus sent this message: "The blind receive their
sight and the lame walk, lepers are cleansed and the deaf
hear, and the dead are raised up, and the poor have good
news preached to them" (Matthew 11:5). There could be no
more telling proof of Jesus' messiahship than this. He meets
people's needs. Need he say more?

The Book of Acts tells the story of how the gospel broke
from Judaic restraints so that every one could understand
the good news. "We hear them telling in our own tongues
the mighty works of God" (Acts 2:11) they exclaimed,
amazed at God's mighty power. The New Testament insists
in its every sentence that Jesus Christ is the truly relevant
one.

It is impossible to miss this persistent theme of accommodation in the incarnation; it is an integral part of the gospel.
Furthermore, the incarnation is not only the way we are
saved from self-destruction, but is the model which the new

people of God employ as they participate with God in his mission in the world. As Jesus accommodated himself to varieties of human need, so we, in him, are enabled to bring a relevant gospel to all people everywhere.

To suggest that the Christian church is not under divine constraint to meet human need in all cultures is completely unacceptable. And if Jesus accommodated himself to any one, he accommodates himself to all. The question, therefore, is not whether accommodation is a biblical reality, but how it works itself out in the life of the church.

Implications for Mission

1. Jesus Christ restores fallen mankind.

We cannot regain our full stature until we return in humble submission to our Creator who, in Christ, is also our Savior. Therefore, good deeds done in the name of Christ, while laudatory, will not correct the fall. People become new creatures only when they find peace with God through Jesus Christ. While the fall did not turn people into stupid, powerless persons, it did make it impossible for them to win God's favor through their own efforts. Salvation is accomplished only through Jesus Christ.

2. The gospel is the result of God's achievement.

All world religions recognize that humankind is out of tune with God and must, therefore, strive to satisfy the God whom they have wronged. They construct elaborate religious systems which they feel will placate the gods which they imagine. In this way these religions try to be relevant to God. The Christian gospel is the other way around. It announces that God has become relevant to our need. God has come down to meet us because we cannot ascend by our own efforts to meet the demands of God. For this reason God's grace is the key factor in evangelism.

3. A correct understanding of the fall is vital.

A theology which discounts the effect of the fall will produce a missiology which will fail to appreciate the absolute necessity of the grace of God. There are such today. They offer only the hope of self-improvement through human striving. A biblical understanding of the fall is a prerequisite for a proper understanding of salvation as offered in Jesus Christ.

2

JESUS, ONE FOR ALL

When my wife and I were visiting churches just before our first term of missionary service in Africa, one dear brother took my hand warmly and said, "Brother Don, we hope you return from Africa just like you are now. Don't change." I was not quite sure what he meant but I had some idea, so I assured him that I shared his sentiments and asked that he please pray for me.

Now as I look back on that conversation, I realize how impossible it is for anyone who is at all sincere in his missionary vocation to keep from changing. In fact, if you do not change you are not going to influence very many people at all.

But what adjustments should you make? How far can or should you bend? When Mennonite missionaries (they are probably no different from others, really) get serious about relating to people in cross-cultural evangelism, they discover how much their thinking, values, self-understanding, and even their identity are tied up with their cultural conditioning. Their problem is complicated because they probably assume that the subculture that they were reared in (the Mennonite communities) is a "Christian culture." It was created by godly people over many decades, therefore it should be good! But that highly prized culture can and usually does become a handicap in relating to people in radically different cultures.

Almost all missionaries get to the point where they encounter this problem like a mountain. Normally they feel hampered by their cultural identity. It is not uncommon to hear the sentiment, "We must abandon our shoofly pie, our cracker box church buildings, and our Anabaptist history if we are going to be a truly missionary church." Missionaries often realize how much ethnicity can become a barrier in evangelism and they are tempted to think that the only way out is to say "good-bye" to cultural roots or identity and to accommodate themselves to the local cultures. But is that the way?

We sympathize with the sincerity of this approach, but is it the way to go about cross-cultural evangelism? At first glance it appears laudable, but when we look at it closely we find it is flawed. To begin with, culture is not like a coat that you put on and take off. It is too much a part of one. It would be more like taking your bones out than taking off a coat. Then, too, what part of the other culture should we incorporate into ourselves and what should we leave out? We could work endlessly at this problem and fail to get the job done.

The apostle Paul looked honestly at his culture and concluded that as far as salvation was concerned it was about as significant as a load of garbage (Philippians 2). Yet he recognized the benefits of having a cultural pedigree like he had. He also warned us about being so proud of our culture that it hinders our fellowship with all Christians.

These thoughts are helpful but we need a broader canvas on which to sketch an understanding of the part culture and "peoplehood" play in cross-cultural evangelism. I find the doctrine of divine election (or is it divine selection?), which runs as a red thread through the Scriptures, to be very helpful. This is such an important concept that we'll get it under our microscope for examination.

Can we agree on the fact that God did have some purpose in preserving us as a brotherhood for these many years? Did he elect or select us for something? I think we can, but we then go on to ask, did he elect us to be separated out or to be involved in the world? If he preserved us for these 450 years, is it not a bit irresponsible, we might ask, to now lose ourselves in mission? Are we for him, as a bride separated out and carefully prepared for her husband, or are we for the world? These are the questions that can either unite or divide us. But we cannot avoid looking honestly at the question.

Called for What Purpose?

A proper understanding of election as seen from the biblical point of view will help us to see that even though we are, in many ways, different or unique because of our history, tradition, and self-understanding, we can still be relevant to human need in cross-cultural evangelism. Just because we were chosen to be "different" does not necessarily say that we were therefore not chosen to be relevant to human need and uninvolved in our world.

We can all agree on the fact that God seeks all people; his salvation is for everyone. To carry this ministry forward God chooses people who live in specific cultures to witness to his universal love. He always worked that way. To preserve the "race" he chose Noah, to establish a covenanted people he chose Abraham, and to announce God's salvation he chose Israel.

This election process reaches its culmination in Jesus Christ who was the one chosen from the foundation of the world, the only begotten of the Father. Jesus Christ, the chosen one, is unique. In fact, if he is not unique there is no salvation for anybody; that is how important the doctrine of election is. Lesslie Newbigin, a missiologist, stated it simply and profoundly when he said,

> Salvation can only be by the way of election. The key to the relation between the universal and the particular is God's way of election. The one (or the few) is chosen for the sake of the many; the particular is chosen for the sake of the universal.[1]

Newbigin anchors the doctrine of election in Creation. The core idea of the creation story, he argues, is that people are not self-sufficient, self-contained, and self-enclosed units; people are relational beings who work out their destiny in community. If salvation is relational, reasons Newbigin, then God, through election, must enter human relationships at a particular point of history in a highly specific, unique way. Salvation is not just an idea or a concept. It is based on historical reality; it actually happened. Jesus Christ took on the form of man and in that form died as the sacrifice for sin. He related to humankind in a specific, historical way.

Jesus Christ, the unique revealer and minister of God's grace, has just the right answer for everyone's needs everywhere and for all time. He gives living bread to the

---

1. Lesslie Newbigin, *The Open Secret* (Grand Rapids: Wm. B. Eerdmans, 1978), p. 85.

hungry, water of life to the thirsty, rest to the weary, forgiveness to the sin-burdened, release to those in chains. Jesus presented himself as *the Man* for everyone. He understood people's needs. Indeed, he experienced those needs from the inside of one culture. He participated fully in that culture.

This is the wonder of the incarnation. God made himself available for all humankind, which means that his salvation is for every person. He became the universal Savior by becoming a particular human being. We many are saved by the one. "As in Adam all die, so also in Christ shall all be made alive" (1 Corinthians 15:22).

The incarnation has validity for all persons, yet was accomplished by one Person. Jesus entered a precise moment in history (in the days of Herod the king), was born in a particular place (Bethlehem of Judea), was nurtured by very human Galilean parents in a little town called Nazareth where he ate the lake's fish and attended the local school. When he began his public ministry, he spoke of the good news first in his own community in their tongue. Jesus entered human life, not as a transcultural being but he entered our life like the rest of us, through a cultural needle's eye. He was born a Galilean, not a German or a Kikuyu, but a Galilean. And that was God's plan. We call that "election."

Jesus did not despise or reject his culture as one might expect him to have done because of the fact that he was the universal Savior. He submitted to tribal conditioning so that he could become the universal Savior. There was no other way (Luke 2:40).

We come to a biblical principle: It is necessary to be particular in order to be universal. Everyone participates in a culture and only a cultural being can relate authentically to another cultural being. This gives us a basic clue in answering the question, "How do we view our own culture?" Is it a positive factor? Are we to preserve it or to lose it? Should we be in the world where we might lose it or should we separate ourselves out from the world lest we become part "of the world?" Should we express solidarity with the dominant cultures around us or should we establish Christian subcultures of our own? Should we come out of our cultural enclaves?

Jesus the Galilean

I was once amused by the wistful statement of a new missionary. "I am determined that I will not present any part of my culture to these people. I will preach only Christ." He actually believed that! He said this in American English (with a Southern accent) as he walked to his shiny, powerful Jeep station wagon. This is something like a trout saying that water might be essential for fish but not for him.

Jesus never tried to disarm his friends with the disclaimer, "Now, my dear ones, for the sake of communicating with you I want you to know that I am not really a Galilean. This is only a mask I wear. I hate this idea of being a Galilean because it keeps me from being the cosmic Savior." On the contrary, his "Galilean-ness" earned him the right to speak as a human. He became particular so that he could be universal.

Mission administrator Nathan Showalter described it thus:[2]

> The universal God expressed himself as a Jewish baby. He declared his solidarity with our experience of family, clan, and nation. In this divine identification with human culture a process of change from inside out was begun. No longer would culture be shaped by law from without. Now the law would be written within (Jeremiah 31). The centripetal mission of Israel which drew proselytes into the Jewish assembly, now became the centrifugal mission of Jesus and a new Israel that would be incarnated in every culture and people.

---

2. In personal correspondence.

But Jesus clearly showed that even though he was "in" Galilee, he was not a prisoner of Galileanism or any other "ism." He reached out to all people just where they were with an appropriate word or a gracious deed.

Jesus Christ presented himself to others as someone, the one, with something to give. He is not a demanding Lord but the Lord of grace. He gives beyond measure. He accepts others willingly and openly. He presented himself as desirable. He built a bridge to each person who had need and then he walked across that bridge with his precious presence. He thereby met actual needs of real people in their local situations.

I recall an African testifying that Jesus is like a big package. As we open the package and unwrap the items we are astounded by what is in there. And we never get to the end of opening this wonderful package. The gospel story reinforces this theme again and again. We can see Jesus himself in the story of the Good Samaritan. He went out of his way to tend to the needs of the unfortunate son of Israel who was so recently beaten and robbed. He went "where he was" and had what was needed; wine for energy, oil for healing, a donkey for transportation, and a shekel for hospitality. He concentrated his whole attention on the needs of that poor fellow (Luke 10).

In that story the lowly Samaritan gave what he had in order to help a "blue blood" Jew, whom he knew despised Samaritans. This is the proper Christian stance, to care enough about the other person in need that culture, tradition, and race do not amount to anything. The beaten Jew could not have cared less what the fellow's culture was. When you are needy you do not ask such questions.

Jesus repeated the whole process when he met Saul on the road to Damascus and then lovingly led him by the hand into life-changing experiences. This encounter set the stage for Paul's own missionary approach. Jesus Christ the Galilean met Saul the Pharisee at a spot in the road which goes from Jerusalem to Damascus. Jesus knew of Saul's inner turmoil, so he gave him peace. To Saul, now Paul, Jesus was always the relevant one. Not only was he relevant to Paul's needs but he was equally relevant to the longings of all Jews and Gentiles alike. Paul's whole being responded with joy to the fact that Jesus Christ was relevant to him, the "chief of sinners," and then to all people in all ages.

Good News for Gentiles

Just as Jesus made himself available to the fringe populations of Israel—the Samaritans and the Syrophoenicians—so the apostles, particularly Peter and Paul, took the gospel to non-Jews. Shortly before Saul's encounter with the risen Lord on the Damascus road, Peter had taken the giant step of obedience and baptized the uncircumcised Cornelius (Acts 10, 11) in the Roman garrison town of Caesarea. Reporting this to the brethren at Jerusalem he said, "If then God gave the same gift to them [Cornelius and his household] as he gave to us when we believed in the Lord Jesus Christ, who was I that I could withstand God?" The reply of the elders was as profound as it was simple: "Then to the Gentiles also God has granted repentance unto life." The ·deed was done. Whether Cornelius was subsequently circumcised or not, we have no knowledge, but the ice was broken; the only condition for salvation is repentance. We are saved by grace and not by the works of the law.

Paul was commissioned to take the gospel to the Gentiles, an assignment which he carried out with amazing vigor. But he encountered the problems of the Judaizers who tried to convince the Gentiles, who had been saved by grace, that in order to really please God they should submit to circumcision and the law. Then, the Judaizers promised, the Gentile believers would be complete. They would be first Christians then Jews, similar to the Jewish believers who were first Jews and then Christians. Everything would still be in place, Jesus would be honored and the law would be maintained.

Paul blasted this theology with all of his persuasive eloquence. He asked the Galatians, "Who has bewitched you?" He knew that if that kind of thinking should prevail, then not only would grace be cheapened but it would place an intolerable cultural encumbrance upon evangelism. Paul was so insistent on this point that when Peter, long after he baptized Cornelius in Caesarea, ate with separatistic Jewish Christians at Antioch but not with Gentile Christians, Paul preached Peter a brotherly sermon on the meaning of grace. He said, "We know that a man is not justified by observing the law, but by faith in Jesus Christ." And with additional similar sentiments he exposed Peter's backsliding. Peter's stance probably played into the hands of those, such as Apollos of Alexandria, whose Christology was defective. Paul was convinced that he had to challenge that incipient heresy. Of course, Peter was simply trying not to offend the Jews to whom he was witnessing of Christ.

The central theme of all of Paul's writings is that anyone anywhere can come directly to Christ and through repentant faith find salvation full and free. There are no cultural prerequisites for salvation—or postrequisites either. Salvation is by grace and that is that!

A Test Case—Ephesus

Paul, the apostle of Jesus Christ, developed relevant theologies in many of his letters, but in none so clearly and eloquently as in his epistle to the Ephesians. The drama unfolds in chapter four. The backdrop to the imagery in chapter four is the commonly-held Greek world-view in which the universe has three layers; the heavenlies on top where the obedient spirits lived, the earthlies under that where we live, and the layer under the earth where evil powers planned their stratagems.

Jesus Christ, writes Paul, came down out of the heavenlies, lived among men in the earthlies, and then descended into the lower parts of the earth where he "took captivity captive." He snatched away the booty which Satan had so painstakingly gathered together and then he went up through the earthlies to the heavenlies where he now sits dispensing gifts, including those which were formerly bound by Satan. He dispenses those gifts according to the needs of the body, the church.

Jesus has something to give. And give he does. So eager is he to give that he promised to fill all believers with everything (Ephesians 1:23). What more can we say? What more can he say?

"Let all come," is the message; he will reject no one who sincerely repents and turns to God. "The Spirit and the Bride say, 'Come,' And let him who hears say, 'Come.' And let him who is thirsty come, let him who desires take the water of life without price" (Revelation 22:17). "He who did not spare his own Son but gave him up for us all, will he not also give us all things with him" (Rom. 8:32)?

Jesus was no stranger to the needs of people because he ministered from among the people. The writer to the Hebrews says, "He is not ashamed to call them brethren" (Hebrews 2:11). Jesus determined to meet people just where they were in their need. He determined to interact with them in their idiom. He made himself so available to them that they could experience him within the context of their own perceptions. Nothing was too much to redeem them back to God. Believers everywhere today witness to him as the one who not only gives gifts but also the one who holds the keys to death and hades (Revelation 1:18).

Returning, then, to the question with which we opened this section, "Can people from one culture be relevant to people of another and, if so, how?" Of course, they can, but they must in all humility submit their cultural advantages to the cross of Jesus Christ just like the apostle Paul did. Writing to the Philippians he said,

> Though I myself have reason for confidence in the flesh also. If any other man thinks he has reason for confidence in the flesh, I have more: circumcised on the eighth day, of the people of Israel, of the tribe of Benjamin, a Hebrew born of Hebrews; as to the law a Pharisee, as to zeal a persecutor of the church, as to righteousness under the law blameless. But whatever gain I had, I counted as loss for the sake of Christ. Indeed I count everything as loss because of the surpassing worth of knowing Christ Jesus my Lord. For his sake I have suffered the loss of all things, and count them as refuse, in order that I may gain Christ. (Philippians 3:4-8)

Even though culture gives us our identity and our worldview, it does not give us salvation. Salvation comes only through Christ. Satan would very much like to lift us up in pride and give us feelings of superiority. He tempts us to think that to be fully human everyone else should be like "us." It is as though we were saying, "Is not the world fortunate to have us as the great example of how to be Christians?" It is this cultural pride which bedevils the communication of the gospel. Yet it is not our culture which gets in the way (in fact, cultural identity is our claim to humanity), but what spoils the process is our *pride* of culture. Even after Paul relegated all those things to the rubbish heap, he remained circumcised, a Benjamite, zealous, and a Hebrew.

It was only after Paul was cleansed of cultural pride that God could trust him to be cultural again. It was as though God said, "Paul, now I give back to you what you were willing to throw away. Use it for my glory and not for your own benefit. Your culture is your link with all humankind. But you should never confuse culture with salvation, never again."

Implications for Mission

1. Christians participate in a variety of cultures.

Culture gives persons identity but it does not lift one group above another. We are saved by grace, not by participating in a "God-fearing" culture. Nor is anyone farther from the kingdom by participating in a culture which has more recently received the gospel. Every culture or nation will cast its crown before the throne of God and the Lamb.

2. Fellowships contain a variety of persons.

Within the fellowship there is no place for human stratification such as that between Jew or Greek, bond or free, male or female, first, second, or third world Christians, powerful or weak. Authentic Christian fellowships include persons from various backgrounds whom Christ has redeemed.

3. Contextualization is a must.

Every fellowship ought to have the right to develop its own worship expression within the context of the local cultural idiom, language, thought pattern, and world-view. This is called "contextualization." At the same time, especially in urban situations or in societies of high mobility, the local fellowship needs to demonstrate in a highly visible way the heterogeneity of the body. Christians ought to accept persons culturally unlike themselves. This demonstrates that cultural affiliation has nothing to do with one's worthiness to be accepted by Christ.

4. *Every church should be a relevant church.*

Each fellowship is responsible for the full expression of the gospel within its community. Christians should help one another but no group should do for another what each can and should be doing.

3

THE GOSPEL
SUITED TO EVERY CULTURE

Let's take a fast-paced trip through church history, beginning with the Acts to the present time, to show how the gospel was received by an amazing variety of cultures. The glimpses into church history will be brief, without much commentary, so that we can comprehend the breadth of God's grace. The theme is always the same: evangelists enter cultures with what they have just like Peter and John did in Acts 3. They saw that lame fellow begging for a handout at the temple gate called "beautiful." His need was quite obvious. Peter turned to him and said, "I give you what I have" (Acts 3:6). We give what we have. Peter and John had the healing Jesus and that was enough by far. But in each of the cases which follow we are astounded to realize the glorious truth that the one gospel fits everybody.

From Jerusalem to Suburbia
Let us begin with the church at Jerusalem, the first Chris-

tian fellowship. What aspect of the gospel was good news to them? It had to do with the Mosaic law. They rejoiced greatly in the fact that Jesus nailed to his cross, as it were, the ordinances written against them, and he died to those ordinances for them (Colossians 2:14). Then they were set free from the fear of the law's condemnation. They discovered that as Christians they could obey the law out of love and no longer because of the fear of death. The good news came to Jerusalem as the answer to the burden of the law.

But not so in bustling, pagan Ephesus. That city knew little of the law of Moses. They specialized in spiritism, exorcisms, and the like. Ephesus was renowned for its occult specialists. There Paul and Silas confronted evil spirits for two and a half years. They healed the sick and cast out evil spirits. People brought handkerchiefs and work aprons to Paul and Silas to get "blessed." These items were then placed on the sick and they were healed. Jesus Christ met the Ephesians just where they were and they responded by acknowledging him as the Lord of the principalities and powers. "Fear fell upon them all; and the name of the Lord Jesus was extolled. Many also of those who were now believers came, confessing and divulging their practices" (Acts 19:17, 18).

Across the bay in Athens Paul interacted with another culture, the Athenian philosophers. Through philosophical deduction the Greeks had concluded that there must be a God who is the Creator, the sustainer of the universe, its first cause. Paul startled them with his announcement that the "unknown God," the first cause, is none other than Jesus Christ of Nazareth, now risen and is "not far from each one of us" (Acts 17:27). The result? "Some men joined him and believed, among them Dionysius the Areopagite and a woman named Damaris and others with them" (Acts 17:34).

Leaping across several centuries to Europe in the Middle Ages, death scourged the land with plagues and pestilences. The people lived in fear of evil powers and in fear of death. These people needed an answer to the horrors of death. Out of this milieu emerged the passion plays of the Middle Ages which announced through drama that Jesus Christ displaces the "evil reaper." This was their cultural expression of what Jesus meant to them. And many people were renewed in their faith by Jesus Christ who destroys the fear of death for them.

By the time of the Reformation, guilt rather than fear was the dominant problem. What a breath of fresh air it was to Northern Europeans of the sixteenth century to discover that no one is saved by merit, but by the grace of God! They clutched to their breasts the knowledge that anyone who depends solely on the finished work of Christ can experience cleansing from sin whether there are priests and bishops present or not.

The Enlightenment followed with its emphasis upon spiritual and intellectual self-betterment. Jesus offered himself as the object of their pious longings. During this era "deeper" life was cultivated by spiritual exercises and disciplines.

Moving to modern times, as missionaries in East Africa, we were impressed by the way Jesus broke right through and met people where they were. For example, he set people free from fear of evil spirits. He also liberated men from male chauvinism, so that monogamy became not only possible, but desirable. He also gave women a new understanding of their worth before God.

About 1970 a situation occurred among a very conservative tribe in East Africa, the Masai. They experienced a type of demon possession which their demon manipulators could not control. Only through Christ and Christian baptism was the possession broken. The good news to them was that Jesus Christ was more powerful than that dreaded demon which they could not control.

Among the Kekchi Indians of Guatemala, the good news is that the alcohol habit can be broken, and that people can live at peace with one another. A sister Indian church encourages people to bring their stomachs to Christ for conversion. A converted stomach, they testify, refuses whiskey.

In a little fellowship near Sydney, Australia, I was touched by the testimony of a newborn Christian who thanked the Lord that since his conversion his electricity bill was going down. Less midnight TV, no doubt.

In middle-class United States the good news comes in the form of a Jesus who affirms the individual, penetrates his loneliness, and puts people back in touch with their own feelings and with one another.

And so it goes. Jesus proves time and time again that he specializes in meeting people just where he finds them and he bows his shoulder to take on their problems.

Sometimes my paternalistic instincts get the best of me and I am tempted to warn Jesus that he might be getting himself into trouble by making himself so readily available. But then I recall my own initial meetings with the Lord. I, too, had profound needs which Jesus Christ alone could meet. He spoke to me when I was sixteen years old in the context of the needs of a sixteen-year-old. But now I am fifty. How Jesus has changed over the years! Yet he remains in all his fullness.

There is no end to the variety of needs which Jesus Christ meets. The list could go on and on. But the weight of the argument is clear; Jesus Christ is well able to meet everyone's needs everywhere at any time. As part of this purpose he enlists cross-cultural missionaries to announce this almost unbelievable fact. For the evangelist, Jesus Christ is ever and always the relevant one.

Assuming that this theological understanding is correct, then missionaries must recognize that Jesus Christ can meet people *where they are.*

The Bible—Its Content and Method

A missionary is driven back to the Bible again and again, not only because of the content of the Bible but because the Bible, particularly the New Testament, is first of all the story of how the gospel went from culture to culture and second, the entire New Testament is itself letters and tracts written by missionary evangelists to present Christ to others.

Each of the writers addressed a particular audience or person. For example, Matthew wrote to convince the Jews that Jesus is the Messiah while Luke, himself a Greek Christian, wrote his gospel and the Acts to convince his friend Theophilus, a fellow Greek, that Jesus is not only the Jewish Messiah but he is also the Savior of Greeks.

John's writings are especially interesting because he introduces Jesus as the "Logos" which existed even before the earth was created. That was a Greek or Hellenistic concept. He is obviously writing for Hellenized Jews. Matthew, on the other hand, writing to "Hebrew" Jews, builds upon the "covenant" idea which the Jews understood well. Approaches will shift depending upon the cultural orientation of the audience.

This concern for making sure the "hearer" really hears has given rise to several quite distinct Christologies in the New Testament. That is, they see Christ from slightly different angles.

Lesslie Newbigin asserts,

It is important for a faithful doing of Christian theology that we should affirm and insist that the New Testament contains not one Christology, but several. This is not an unfortunate defect to be regretted or concealed. It is, on the contrary, of the essence of the matter because it makes clear the fact that Christology is always to be done *in via* (on the way) at the interface between the gospel and the cultures which it meets on its missionary journey. It is of the essence of the matter that Jesus was not concerned to leave as a fruit of his work a precise verbatim record of everything he said and did, but that he was concerned to create a community which would be bound to him in love and obedience, learn discipleship even in the midst of sin and error, and be his witness among all peoples. If there were to be discovered in the New Testament one definitive Christology framed in the 'ipsissima verba' of Jesus himself, the consequence would be that the gospel would be forever bound absolutely to the culture of first century Palestine. The variety of Christologies actually to be found in the New Testament is part of the fundamental witness to the nature of the gospel.[1]

Christologies are in reality the way Christ is perceived by different cultures. It is impossible to even imagine anyone trying to say anything about Jesus Christ in a cultural vacuum.

More Help Available from Social Sciences

There is an increased awareness on the part of missionaries that they should take this matter of accommodation more seriously than they have done. One of the reasons that this is possible is that missionaries are now utilizing a variety of rather newly developed disciplines as they strive to make the gospel more relevant. The following exemplify this.

---

1. Lesslie Newbigin, *The Open Secret* (Grand Rapids: Wm. B. Eerdmans, 1978), p. 176.

a. Anthropology

To begin with, cultural anthropology, which is the study of man as a communal creature, provides some very helpful insights. That discipline helps us to see that if we enter another's world we should have some understanding of what that world is. Every missionary can now collect a whole shelf of books and periodicals by Christian anthropologists. These were simply not available fifty years ago.

b. Communications

An entire new science has come into being called the communication sciences. This discipline helps in the process of taking a message from one culture and introducing it to another culture without loss of meaning. This is a very important aid in missionary work. Now missionaries talk about code stores, encoding, decoding, code glossaries, and of feedback.

c. Pedagogy

Pedagogy is a sophisticated word for teaching. The pedagogists insist that what is taught must relate to what the people already know. We discover that a lot of what we teach so faithfully has very little impact on life because we do not always connect with where people are.

The definition of God in the Westminster Confession comes to mind to illustrate this point. It proceeds thus, "God is infinite in being and perfection, a most pure spirit, invisible, without body, parts or passion, immutable, immense, eternal, incomprehensible, almighty, most wise, most holy, most free, most absolute." This confession made a lot of sense to the people who wrote it. We know this because we have record of their great debates. But it is of limited value as a part of the catechetical instruction for Kikuyu believers in Kenya, for example, where the Presbyterians are strong.

Theological education in most of the third world really originates in the West. Textbooks are often written in other cultures for their own consumption and are not, therefore, particularly relevant in the third world. And when books do appear in the local languages they are often little more than translations from a European language. It amazes me that there is so little variation around the world in the method and content of formal theological education even though there are massive differences in the world's cultures. The pedagogists tell us that something is wrong here. What is taught and how it is taught must reflect the world of the students. We have all heard of scratching where it does not itch. This characterizes much theological education in the world, especially among the newer churches.

Other valuable disciplines could be added, all of which help missionaries come to a deeper understanding of the process of evangelism across cultures. Good missionary training now includes the insights of the social sciences and the humanities as a matter of course. It is hoped that this determination to be more accommodating to local needs will produce approaches which are more helpful.

The Church Growth Movement

The Church Growth movement is an outstanding example of missions taking the learnings of the social sciences seriously. They insist that every missionary should spend much time and effort in learning about local cultures. The proponents of this movement view the world as a mosaic of "cultures." Their basic assumption is that missions should concentrate on bringing these "cultures" to Christ and then after a comparatively short period of discipling the church should be encouraged to work out their own style of church life and worship in light of the Scriptures. It is imperative, therefore, that each group should have the Bible in their native tongue. It follows that the primary task of missions is to cross the cultural boundaries which divide the mosaics and plant churches which fit each mosaic piece. When it is certain that the church is established in a particular culture, and that they have the Scriptures in their language, the missionaries then should move on. The task of "perfecting" the church is primarily the responsibility of the emerging churches and not of the missionary.

In this way, they contend, mission resources are not tied up in a few places for a long period of time but are released to enter more pieces of the mosaic. More than half of the people on earth, the Church Growth proponents keep reminding us, are in cultural mosaics where there are no effective evangelistic churches. So, if the world is to be evangelized, missions should disengage as much as possible from the "perfecting" ministries and move on. The Church Growth method takes seriously the enormity of the task of bringing the gospel to every creature, and tries to do something about it. It also takes seriously the need to be culturally relevant.

Summary

We are becoming more aware of the fact that the missionary mandate which is to witness cross-culturally is a very complicated business. To illustrate, a Yugoslavian visiting the United States read the headline, "Reds Massacre Yankees." Immediately he wondered where the Russians were killing Americans. It was only after he read further that he discovered it was simply a baseball game, a sport of which Americans are fond.

For the work of missionaries to be successful they must be constantly aware of the fact that they are trying to communicate the great good news across cultural boundaries. They use every means available so that they, as Paul, can become "all things to all men."

Implications for Mission

1. Jesus is appropriate for all cultures.

Those persons who are called and gifted for cross-culture evangelism and mission should be encouraged to present Christ as the one who can and will meet the felt needs of the people. There is no culture whose needs will exhaust the Trinity. It is in this assurance that missionaries go forward.

2. Mennonite evangelism is usually cross-cultural.

Owing to the fact that the Mennonite Church assumed an ethnic identity to some degree over its four-century history, when the church evangelizes its neighbors today, it is in fact engaging in cross-cultural missions right at home. This puts certain strains on the fellowships. Were the church more like society at large, this would not pose as difficult a problem.

3. Theology is formulated locally.

Local fellowships or groups of fellowships should take responsibility for interpreting the gospel in their own setting. As the church spreads out across the world, the need for such local interpretation becomes even more evident. It is not appropriate for one fellowship to lord it over another but neither is it right for any fellowship to disregard the insights and understandings of sister fellowships throughout the world. The same principle applies within fellowships where individual consciences may differ.

4. The social sciences are subservient to the Holy Spirit.

The church should use the resources of the social sciences, but it should never rely on the methodology of those disciplines to replace the redemptive work of the Holy Spirit.

4

PITFALLS OF THEOLOGIES
OF ACCOMMODATION

The gospel is one; on this point we can all agree. There are not two gospels or three. As Paul puts it, there is not a gospel of Apollos, another of Peter, and another of Christ. The gospel is the gospel. We have "one Lord, one faith, one baptism, one God and Father of us all, who is above all and through all and in all" (Ephesians 4:5-6). The gospel is not something which *we* own, it is God's work and is therefore *his*. We participate in it by faith.

Theology, however, is a human means to understand and interpret the gospel. Christians bring their needs, their hopes, their way of comprehending reality to the Scriptures, and under the guidance of the Holy Spirit find answers to their questions, and, incidentally, find new questions.

The point I wish to make is that every theology is an attempt to apply the gospel to actual and varied life situations. If theology is viewed in this way, then we are always involved in the process of developing our theology because our needs keep changing and our societies continue to change. The result might well be that the theology of one culture does not speak directly to the heartfelt concerns of another culture. Many missionaries are not fully aware of this fact.

This chapter lifts out a few of the more recent theologies. Of the formulating of theologies there is no end. It seems that as soon as one appears and we begin to understand it, then another comes along. But we should not be dismayed because no theology is "the last word." We must remember that theology must be relevant if it is to be helpful at all.

We will identify a few of these newer theologies, noting their strong points and their basic appeal and then draw some conclusions about the promise and dangers of the whole process.

Theologies of Liberation

One of the most talked about "new" theologies is liberation theology. This has emerged where poor, underprivileged, or subservient people begin to feel that they are little more than charity cases for the world's rich. This urge to be free is deeply imbedded in the human spirit. There is a feeling abroad in our time that freedom is a birthright and those who are not politically and economically free should struggle to get free.

When the oppressed people happen to be Christians they often become enthralled by the liberation theme of the Scriptures. They see that God, too, is interested in liberation; in fact, they see in him their liberator. The great Exodus passages form the core of their theology. But they see the liberation theme everywhere. For instance, when Jesus appeared on the scene, he announced his Messiahship in the context of liberation: "He [God] has anointed me to preach good news to the poor. He has sent me to proclaim release to the captives ... to set at liberty those who are oppressed"

(Luke 4:18). The privileged peoples of the earth find it easy to spiritualize this text, but the underprivileged take it literally.

If Jesus does meet people at their point of need, he will certainly appear to these people as the one who will set them free. These people are often joined by missionaries who theologize with them about their problems and their dreams. Out of this context liberation theologies arise which have enormous appeal. Latin America and South Africa are particularly amenable to this new theology because in those areas a huge and intolerable economic gap exists between the rich and the poor. The poor can scarcely believe that God wants it that way. They long for liberation and their theology reflects this hope.

Economic Development Theologies

In communities where political liberty exists, but where the lack of economic development bedevils the people, there Jesus is seen as the one who is concerned that his people have enough money to buy food, send their children to school, that they have roads, pit latrines, and the like. These people, and compassionate people who are committed to helping them, are drawing the outlines of theologies of development. They elevate the themes of human wholeness, they point to the intolerable inequity between the richer and the poorer nations in the world, and they involve themselves in the problems of political ideology. They are convinced that the Jesus who came to save is also concerned about economics, government, physical well-being, and education.

Ethnic Theologies

Upon conversion to Christ, persons in minority communities who feel pushed aside by powerful, dominating majorities discover liberation which helps them maintain their dignity. They begin to realize that Jesus puts new meaning into their lives because he cares about them right where they are. In addition to releasing them from feeling inferior, he encourages them to accept their roots with gratitude. And so theologies of human dignity or ethnic consciousness are being written in which Jesus is portrayed as interested in people as ethnic beings. Jesus joins them in their singing, so to speak. He encourages them to share their faith in forms which their not-yet-believing neighbors can readily understand.

Renewal Theologies

It often happens in the history of the church that renewal movements break forth. The winds of the Holy Spirit blow at God's pleasure. We are often at a loss to know why it happens at one place and time and not another, but believers do get revived through renewal movements. These are especially blessed times and their effects are often very substantial. Unfortunately, these renewal movements often become concretized in cultural forms peculiar to the setting in which they occurred. The Mennonite Church which resulted from the Anabaptist spiritual renewal is a good illustration of this process.

As Paul put it, "Having begun with the Spirit, are you now ending with the flesh?" (Galatians 3:3). No movement is free from the temptation to become legalistic. Theologies of accommodation come to the rescue and provide a way to break through the legalism by distinguishing between form and essence. The meaning, it is stressed, can be maintained even if the form is modified.

When a denomination, which simply lives in the legalistic remnants of a past revival, discovers that Jesus can meet them just like he met those who began the movement, they experience a joy and an openness which changes the nature of their discipleship. In this way Jesus becomes highly relevant.

When these people write their theologies, they make connections between their own awakening and that of their "founders." These are theologies which provide rationale for changing outmoded forms in favor of the new on the basis of the fact that what really matters is the work of the Holy Spirit in the life of the group and not simply copying the forms of a long-gone movement.

Nativistic Theologies

As the gospel penetrates the hundreds of cultures around the world, nativistic theologies are emerging. The five thousand or so Independent denominations in Africa are a good example of this phenomenon. They insist on proving that Jesus is not a foreigner and that Christianity is not a foreign religion. So they deliberately localize their faith. They are actually formulating accommodating theologies. What results is often a hodgepodge of new and old, of East and West, but it is at least an absorbing attempt to contextualize Christianity.

Dialogical Theologies

There is little doubt that Western Christian missionaries have often confronted the religions of the world in a head-on fashion. This has proved to be quite ineffective when the clash was between Christians and Muslims or Hindus or similar religions which can boast a glorious religious history. Within recent years missiologists seek to discover how God is already active in the communities which have not yet believed in Jesus Christ. One missionary put it recently,

"We do not take Jesus there; he is already there. We go to meet him through those people." If this is one's theology, then the dialogical method is fine because through dialogue Christ can be discovered. The other benefit of dialogue is that it takes the strident, imperializing, worldly triumphalism out of mission and replaces it with a more humble stance.

Theologies of Accommodation Analyzed

It is clear that concentrating on accommodation is consistent with the incarnational model of Jesus Christ. He became "the man" for "all people." He gave himself to bear the burden of people everywhere. A missionary community of faith must meet the not-yet-believing community at its point of need with the promise that there is a loving Savior and Lord whose limitless resources are available for its particular needs.

However, the theologies of accommodation are fraught with pitfalls, some of which we do well to recognize lest we find ourselves too much "of" the world.

a. "Ideolatry"

Jesus does reveal himself to people in such a way that he undoubtedly accommodates himself to meet their basic needs. While this is exemplary, it is also very dangerous because people tend to fit Jesus into their "isms." An "ism" is an ideological or theoretical framework already present in the not-yet-believing community whose presuppositions are based upon authorities which conflict with or even supersede the authority of Jesus Christ. A prevalent "ism," for example, is nationalism. Christians live in nations and they should support their governments, but blind allegiance to nationalism leads to apostasy. And so it is with other "isms." The danger with "isms" is that of idolatry of ideas, or "ideolatry."

In this regard liberation theology is highly perilous. Classical liberation theology assumes the validity of the Marxist praxis philosophy which undergirds communism's theories. If praxis philosophy works in economics, the argument goes, then why not use it as the category in which theology is done? That sounds fine but an example will highlight how easy it is to flirt with heresy. Marxist philosophy insists that the truth must be done. This sounds very Christian because Christians also believe that it is essential to "do the truth" (1 John 1:6). The catch is that in Marxist philosophy truth does not exist *at all* except in the deed. "There is no truth outside or beyond the concrete historical events in which men are involved as agents."[1] To the communist it is unthinkable that truth predates human existence. Jesus' assertion, "I am the truth," is an inconceivable idea to classical Marxists. In the last analysis the ideological framework may, and often does, take precedence over the gospel itself.

b. Ethnocentrism

A second weakness follows closely on the first. Every culture sees itself as holding to *the* correct view of the universe; all other world views, as a consequence, are considered to be inferior. This can, and often does, result in the universalization or sacralization of one's own philosophy or culture. A Swahili proverb says, "The water in a piece of gourd is the ant's ocean."

This kind of an attitude leads to false assumptions such as, "If Jesus Christ reveals himself in a way that my culture can

---

1. Miguez Bonino, *Revolutionary Theology Comes of Age* (London: S.P.C.K., 1975), p. 72.

understand him with such blessed clarity, then others will see him clearly if they can see him through *our* world-view." Assuming this to be true, therefore, part of the process of evangelism is to make others like we are. This leads to cultural imperialism in the name of evangelization. We missionaries have had to struggle with this temptation for years. We also fall prey to the tantalizing thought that the Western scientific world-view is particularly blessed and affirmed by God; after all, we have accomplished some heroic feats such as landing a man on the moon. We easily fall into one trap or another. Slowly and painfully we begin to see that we all preach not only Christ, but we preach Christ *as we understand him*. We run not only the risk of cultural imperialism, or ethnocentrism, but we run the risk of repelling those who are unlike ourselves. A final tragedy is that if others should become like us, then there is little reason to learn from them.

c. *Status Quo Stagnation*

A third weakness is that when accommodation is emphasized there is often a tendency to accept without question the cultural status quo. In this case the gospel is fashioned to conform to what is already there. A gospel which only and always says yes to one's culture must be a weak counterfeit of the real thing. It supports static concepts which are less revolutionary than is warranted by the gospel message.

We often hear the question, "How can we indigenize the gospel?" The basic weakness of the "indigenization" approach to missiology is that it assumes too often that the gospel is less revolutionary than it actually is. This weakness appears now and again in the Church Growth movement because it emphasizes the planting of churches which are truly continuous with their cultures. Certainly the gospel of

Jesus Christ is more revolutionary than that. The Church Growth movement is maturing, but its greatest weakness is that missionaries and evangelists which make more than they should of the "homogenous" principle, an aspect of anthropology which is dear to their hearts, may be encouraging churches to isolate themselves against outside influences and to concentrate too much on building "ethnic" churches.

Any theology which concentrates its major attention on points of entry, bridges of grace, felt needs, and so on, must guard against becoming a domesticated and, therefore, ineffectual part of the "old order."

d. Ethical Relativism

Concentrating on accommodation can result in the perpetuation of human barriers rather than on their removal. If Jesus Christ is at home among us, goes the reasoning, it is because he approves of our culture. If so, then he is with us in our aspirations, our goals, and our way of achieving these goals. There must be something wrong, for example, with a missiology which undergirds the policy of racial superiority as it is practiced some places in our world. In contrast, one is reminded of the disgust with which many nineteenth-century missionaries viewed slavery. Missionaries and all Christians, for that matter, must discern evil in all cultures, even those which pronounce themselves "Christian."

e. Evangelistic Lethargy

Accommodation theologies can, and often do, blunt the cutting edge of evangelism. A dialogical approach to evangelism is sometimes employed instead of evangelization which holds to the uniqueness of Jesus Christ. While dialogue is essential in any meaningful communication, evangelism which says little more than, "I affirm the beautiful

things about your faith and I expect reciprocal appreciation," is not really being honest to the claims which Jesus
Christ made for himself.

f. Isolation

Accommodation theologies tend to be localized theologies, suitable only for them. While this follows naturally,
local churches must guard against isolating themselves from
the world church. Ethnic theologies too often result in little
more than "folk religions." In this case tribal gods reappear
and the culture becomes synonymous with the church.

g. Theological Legalism

Missionaries usually assume that as the people study the
Scriptures they will grow and mature in their Christian faith.
This is an admirable, but all too often, false hope. Often
people harden into their initial theological understandings and
they remain there "world without end. Amen." We have
plenty of examples of this in the history of the church. The
Church Growth movement struggles with this issue.

h. Syncretism

An additional obvious pitfall is syncretism. When non-
Christian assumptions dilute the gospel to the point that the
essential message is compromised, then harmful syncretism
results. History can lead us to the graveyards of many well-
intentioned churches which went the syncretistic route.
Jesus was right when he insisted that a person cannot serve
two masters (Matthew 6). On the other hand, some Christians fear syncretism so much that they are paralyzed and
simply carry on with business as usual, blissfully unaware of
the fact that their own theology is itself biased toward their
own world-view.

i. Theological Relativism

Theologies of accommodation tend to be uncomfortable with the concept of the "giveness" of the gospel. They prefer, rather, to highlight the relative nature of reality. They cringe before phrases like "the core of the gospel," "propositional or normative truth," "the essence of the gospel." They feel that any reductionism is ultimately determined by one's culture and, therefore, should be avoided. They eschew any fundamentalism.

This is especially true of what has come to be called "modernism" which is essentially an attempt to accommodate the gospel to a scientific mind-set in the West for which the supernatural seems no longer an appropriate category. This might have been a valiant effort to evangelize secularized people, but it floundered on the rock of relativism.

Summary

Lest I give the impression that theologies of accommodation are so dangerous that we should avoid them like the plague, I must hasten to say that we are duty-bound to run the risks of accommodation for the sake of evangelism. Jesus did just that; he became a Galilean Jew, running the risk that Christianity would be no more than a culture-bound, Nazarite sect within Galilean Judaism. But it did not. The Holy Spirit was given to that little brotherhood in such measure that within thirty years after the ascension, the gospel had sprung free from its Jewish cultural trappings and was on the way to becoming the good news for all people.

It is a risk indeed to accommodate the gospel to particular people's unique needs; however, not to do so because of the risk of potential syncretism is not even an option. That would be an exercise in unbelief. A leading Dutch theologian, Visser't Hooft, former General Secretary of the World

Council of Churches, said it well: "Our desire to arrive at a truly adequate communication of the gospel must be stronger than our fear of syncretism."[2]

I am eternally grateful that Jesus Christ met me and continues to meet me at my point of need—often in a way I would not have imagined or even preferred—but he is always there. Jesus Christ as the Good Samaritan continues to come where we are, with the wine, the oil, the donkey, and the money, all of which are placed at our disposal. But above all he meets us in love and in turn enables us to so love others that we can meet them at their point of need.

We are reminded of that beautiful picture of God's accommodating grace in Revelation 21. The river is still running from beneath the throne of God and the Lamb. The tree of life is flourishing with fruit for each month of need and with leaves which hold balm for the healing of every bruise and sore of every nation on earth (Revelation 22).

New Testament theology is, therefore, concerned with Christ's accommodating grace. All people are entitled to experience God's redemption in their local idiom.

Biblical Anabaptist theology applauds the efforts of the theologians of accommodation, realizing that the gospel of Jesus Christ is for all. This aspect of our theology is gaining prominence because of the renewed awareness of the missionary mandate. It would be unwise for the brotherhood, nevertheless, to so encourage the theologies of accommodation as to disregard the theologies of radical departure from or nonconformity to our "age." We should be as committed to evangelism as we are to the nurture of the saints. We are, indeed, in the world even though we are not of the world.

---

2. W. A. Visser't Hooft, *No Other Name* (Philadelphia: The Westminster Press, 1963), p. 124.

Implications for Mission

1. Christians avoid religious syncretism culture in Christianity.
To be human is to be cultural. The gospel must be expressed in cultural forms, although the gospel message transcends all cultures. Each culture has features which are antagonistic to Christ, but on the other hand each one has features which enhance the graces Christ affirms. Instructed by the Scriptures and quickened by the Holy Spirit, the believing community will bring the light of the gospel to bear upon the evil and the good in their culture. But they must beware of syncretism. The perils of religious syncretism are real. But this is a problem for all Christian fellowships, not only for new ones.

2. God reveals himself somewhat in world religions.
We believe that the church is called to witness to Jesus Christ and to urge others to believe in him regardless of the apparent beauty of their non-Christian religious system. We believe that the Holy Spirit is already working outside the church and within other world religions, preparing people to hear and receive the gospel of Jesus Christ. That witness to truth within the religious systems is sometimes only faintly present. Often the sinfulness of man perverts the truth, and religion itself may become a form of rebellion against God. Yet the witness of the Holy Spirit is always there.

3. Salvation is through Christ alone.
Whenever the gospel is proclaimed and lived within any religious tradition, we can expect that some will believe in Christ and become part of the redeemed community, the church. The testimony of the Bible and of those who have experienced salvation in Christ, is that salvation is found in no one else, "for there is no other name under heaven given among men by which we must be saved" (Acts 4:12). World religions do not give salvation. Salvation is experienced only through Christ.

4. Christians should worship in their own idioms.

Every Christian fellowship ought to experience the living presence of Christ in its own idiom. Their worship and life together will reflect their ethnic character. Where the local fellowship includes more than one culture, all participants should be made to feel "at home."

5

CHRIST CONFRONTS

The Healer Carries a Sword

We delight in the fact that Jesus Christ comes into our experience and meets us there. He is as close to us as breath itself. As he meets my need, so he wants to meet the needs of everybody. Having said that about Jesus, we have certainly not said everything because he is not simply a gratuitous "need meeter." Some people think of him that way and even treat him as though he is the eternal dispenser of goodies. Jesus is God in the flesh and people can never manipulate him to meet their demands. The fact that he is the servant of all does not make everyone his Lord.

I am especially fond of the story of Jesus' interaction with the two on the way to Emmaus. Following Jesus' crucifixion these two lonely figures made their way toward the village of Emmaus, disappointed, distraught, and sad (Luke 24). The one on whom they had pinned their hopes, Jesus of Nazareth, was dead, and their hopes seemed to die with him.

Presently they were joined by an unknown traveler. Out of a spirit of hospitality (or was it out of need for companionship?), they invited him in to their home to spend the night. He accepted their warm invitation. They prepared an evening meal and asked him to join them. They must have been startled by the fact that Jesus, the guest, took the bread, thus assuming the position as host or head of the table. He blessed the bread and gave it to his hosts! He assumed the role which was rightfully his. It was Jesus Christ, the risen Lord. He was invited in as a guest to meet an immediate human need (loneliness, confusion, and depression), but he assumed his proper place as the host, the Lord of the table.

Those two sad, dejected people, upon discovering that their "guest" was in reality the risen Jesus, had no problem acknowledging him as Lord of their table. His presence and self-revelation set energy in motion. That night yet they ran the seven miles back into Jerusalem (uphill, at that) to tell the other disciples what had happened. Their lives would never be the same again. And so it continues to happen: Jesus Christ enters our lives and our homes as a welcome guest, but he does not remain a pampered guest very long. He moves inevitably to the head of the table where he rightfully belongs. Of course, we can then dethrone him if we want to, but his rightful place is clearly at the head of the table. In fact, there is no other place for him. Someone noted correctly that either Jesus is Lord of all or he is not Lord at all. When Jesus is around, he takes over and changes things. For some this is a problem, for others it is their only hope.

So far we have mainly emphasized that Jesus accommodates himself to meet human needs. He bows his shoulder, so to speak, to bear our burdens. Now we talk of his lordship. What is the truth? Is he for the world which he created or is he against it?

We stand before a paradox. Did Jesus come to the world to bring peace or a sword? He was not too clear at this point, perhaps. In the Sermon on the Mount as recorded in Matthew, he said, "Blessed are the peacemakers, for they shall be called sons of God" (Matthew 5:9). He is very much for making peace. To his disciples he confided in the upper room, "Peace I leave with you; my peace I give to you" (John 14:27). That sounds straightforward, does it not? We are to bring peace where there is hostility, healing where there are wounds.

But Jesus also talked about confrontation and trouble. Early on in his ministry, when he sent his disciples to preach to Israel, he said,

> I send you out as sheep in the midst of wolves. . . . Do not think that I have come to bring peace on earth; I have not come to bring peace, but a sword. For I have come to set a man against his father, and a daughter against her mother, and a daughter-in-law against her mother-in-law; and a man's foes will be those of his own household. Matthew 10:16, 34-36.

This is language of a different sort.

We are caught up short when we realize that it is the same Jesus Christ who binds together and who cuts things apart. He sharpened the dilemma for us, "If you were of the world, the world would love its own; but because you are not of the world . . . therefore the world hates you" (John 15:19).

Jesus Is Radical

Having concentrated in the earlier chapters on the way Jesus Christ meets people at their point of need, we move to a consideration of the radical, revolutionary nature of the gospel of Jesus Christ. While Jesus does affirm many good things in our cultures, he also confronts those anti-Christian attitudes and expressions which exist. No theology of mission is complete without a clear understanding of the way in which the church confronts society.

The gospel is confrontational. In Mennonite circles this aspect of the gospel has often been called nonconformity, arising from the apostle Paul's admonition, "Do not be conformed to this world but be transformed by the renewal of your mind" (Romans 12:2). Jesus accommodates himself to the needs of people but he also confronts society. It is like two parallel tracks which never seem to converge. If confrontation theology is taken to its logical conclusion, it demands that Christians separate themselves from their societies and become counter cultures. If accommodation theology is taken to its logical conclusion, it results in an "invisible" Christianity like salt is invisible in soup. You cannot tell where the salt ends and the soup begins. Is there any way to make sense of all this?

Getting back to the scriptural basis for theologies of confrontation, Paul insisted that Christians must be different. He told the Roman believers, "Don't let the world around you squeeze you into its own mold" (Romans 12:2, Phillips).

It is significant that at Pentecost the signs of the coming of the Holy Spirit are change symbols. The sound as of rushing, mighty wind which announced his coming is not exactly a description of a cozy summer breeze; it is rather a strong symbol of dynamic force, producing change through confrontation. Fire, likewise, is confrontational, because it cannot enter anything without changing it fundamentally. Human tongues were changed so that the good news could leap across cultures like fire leaps from tree to tree in a forest. And then to really dramatize the change which occurred the believers who came from a great number of tribes or nations were so changed that they wanted to eat together in one another's homes. The Holy Spirit is clearly in the business of confronting things as they are and then changing them.

There can be little doubt that Jesus Christ among his people confronts "this age." This is a recurring theme in the Scriptures.

Two Kingdoms Clash

The confrontation aspects of the gospel arise out of the nature of the gospel itself; while Jesus Christ is victorious over Satan, the enemy is still very active seducing people to reject the gospel. These two forces or kingdoms are in conflict with one another, for one is ruled by God, the other by Satan. This can be illustrated by reference to Paul's encounter at Ephesus (Acts 19). Paul and Silas preached Christ in the shadows of both the temple dedicated to Artemis (Diana) and the Ephesian pantheon which housed the local gods. How would Jesus reveal himself in this center of occult worship? He did it by presenting himself through the ministry of Paul and Silas as the healer, in fact a more effective healer than the local "deities." He met the people of Ephesus in an idiom with which they were familiar and with demonstrations of power which they understood. Jesus accommodated himself to their understanding of the world.

But that is not the end of the story. In fact, it is just the beginning. Jesus Christ is not simply a "miraculous" healer, he is Jesus Christ, God among people, the Creator of the universe, the name which is above every other name—in heaven, in the earth, and under the earth—the one who conquered Satan. Furthermore, his name is above all names—past, present, or future (Ephesians 1:21). As such he is above the principalities and powers, the personalities, and even the structures of evil (Ephesians 6:12). Before him, Paul asserts, every knee shall bow and every tongue shall acknowledge that this is a true description of the way things in fact are (Philippians 2:9-11). Jesus is who he said he is.

Who Is This Jesus?

The apostle Paul was not prepared to present Jesus Christ as merely a dispenser of physical healing but he insisted that Jesus of Nazareth is none other than Lord of all, above all, and in a collision course with the devil and the spirits of evil. This is a proclamation and not a speculation. It was not to be argued but either accepted or rejected. What will they do with this claim? If Jesus is Lord of all, what place has he in their traditional gallery of gods? Where does Jesus fit in?

They had to make a decision on this point. They had several options. They could simply reject the claims that Jesus Christ made for himself through the ministry of Paul. To be sure, the miracles done in his name were extraordinary but, after all, they could have concluded, there are many workers of miracles. Even the devil can perform a certain amount of them. Seeing signs does not necessarily mean that a person must change religious convictions. A person can simply say, "But Diana is still good enough for me."

A second option open to them was to place Jesus Christ in the community's pantheon alongside the other deities. The Ephesians were very tolerant and eclectic. They saw no difficulty in worshiping a variety of gods. Each god was helpful in a certain way. Diana, for example, promised fecundity, Jesus Christ promised forgiveness of sins, Caesar promised peace; why not, therefore, embrace all and receive the benefits of each?

This eclectic approach is not a new one. Many Christians, weary of their guilt and sin, like that part of the gospel which promises forgiveness of sins and assurance of salvation but they stop short of acknowledging him as Lord. They end up with a distorted view of reality and therefore can not really comprehend the gospel in its fullness. They limp along as Christians with just enough Christianity to make them miserable.

The third solution is to enthrone Jesus Christ in life just like he is in heaven, "far above all rule and authority and power and dominion, and above every name that is named, not only in this age but also in that which is to come" (Ephesians 1:21).

In order to truly enter into the fullness of Christ, a person must deliberately and willfully give Jesus full and ultimate authority in life. As John the Revelator saw it, we place our crowns before him who alone is King.

Everyone must eventually ask the question which the crowds asked one day, "Is this one collaborating with Beelzebub (the prince of the demons) or is he Beelzebub's conqueror?" (Luke 11). He cannot be both. But he casts out demons. He could do that in collaboration with Beelzebub. But if he is Beelzebub's conqueror, then that makes a fantastic difference! Who is this Jesus anyway? It makes little difference what we might speculate. That does not change one mite who he is. If we acknowledge his lordship and structure our whole lives around him, we become changed people.

For the Ephesians it did not simply mean that Christians sang new little choruses and had nice tea parties. It meant nothing less revolutionary than that masters began to reorganize their relationship with their servants because their "Master also is in heaven" (Ephesians 6:9). It meant that husbands began to relate to wives like Jesus relates to his beloved church. Now that is radical! Instead of Jesus accommodating his wishes to ours, we submit joyfully to his.

By elevating Jesus Christ to his exalted place as King of kings and Lord of lords, a change occurs in the character of all relationships. And that is confrontational.

Conversion Is Confrontational

When people believe in Jesus Christ and place their faith in him, they become new creatures. This shift in allegiance has to be shown. This does not always follow the same pattern for people everywhere or even for two people in the same cultural situation. One of the problems we all have, one which is even more complex for missionaries, is how do you know when a person is converted? What are the telltale proofs? The question is much easier to ask than to answer.

To begin with, conversion is the process of turning away from something and turning toward another. This happens in any culture. However, where the church is first forming, the believers tend to reinforce their conversion by deliberately turning away from the world in which they formerly participated; they confront their societies with vigor. They often refuse to have anything to do with those aspects of their culture which they consider to be unregenerated or downright harmful.

As a missionary in East Africa, I soon discovered that the believers simply refused to engage in any rituals which had to do, even remotely, with the ancestral spirits. Only with great difficulty could they bring themselves to attend traditional funerals or the traditional puberty rituals because these rituals were clearly a part of the ancestor cult. Yet social pressure almost demanded that they appear at least sometime during the event. I found it interesting that even the paraphernalia employed in the former rituals connected with the ancestral spirits were often rejected by the Christians. I was one of those missionaries who fussed because drums were not used in regular church but I see now that I was a bit impatient. It has taken a long time for the people to "launder" drums of their association with pre-Christian ritual. Now drums are used in many churches; however, some older Christians still squirm a little when drums are played in church because they recall the time when drums were contaminated with pre-Christian associations.

Assessing Conversion

Getting back to our major point, first-generation Christians usually confront their pre-Christian culture because they believe that Christian conversion is very radical. They turn their backs on many aspects of their own culture and all too often incorporate many of the symbols and rituals brought by foreigners, thus serving to widen the gap even more between themselves and their societies.

As Christian communities develop and mature in their respective cultures, they usually soften their confrontationist stance and allow for more interaction with their cultures. Having made the point that they are "different," they then slowly begin to concentrate on building bridges to the culture which they had originally rejected.

People who are converted during this phase are expected to be respectable citizens as well as keen Christians and, therefore, conversion is less confrontational than it was during the first-generation phase.

Now and again one finds a distinct subculture developing as a result of conversion, a subculture which persists from generation to generation. These people carry in their very symbolic and ritual system a perpetual reminder of the group's confrontational nature. This is true of many religious orders; the Amish, Hutterites, and Orthodox Jews come quickly to mind. In these situations when individuals are converted, the religious community expects persons to "join" them, to become submissive to their discipline and lifestyle. In a sense, they domesticate the convert. But their style is essentially confrontational in relation to the dominant culture. In this case conversion is more like a puberty ritual through which one passes in order to be a member of a subculture or "tribe."

So we are hard-pressed to describe a real conversion because the situations differ so much. The point is, people get converted in a multitude of sociological situations and, therefore, signs of true conversion tend to differ. Josiah Muganda, a Tanzania Mennonite, noted that

> The American Mennonites have their symbols that were adopted by them at a particular time and place in their history. They do not mean much to Africans. So we might share this same faith and beliefs in such things as peace and nonviolence and love, for there are biblical principles. However, if nonconformity to them (American Mennonites) means noncooperation with other Christians belonging to different denominations, to the African nonconformity would mean things like not going to the juju, the palm reader, or commercial spiritual advisers.[1]

How Radical Conversion?

We may well ask: Is conversion so relative, then, that it is devoid of any central reality? Are there any norms at all? Of course there are. True "conversion" is always radical because the way of Christ always clashes, to some extent, with the ways of humans. But conversion has many expressions and one culture should not be too quick to judge another.

---

1. Josiah Muganda, *The Impact of the Mennonite Mission on Mara Region, Tanzania, 1934-1967* (unpublished MA thesis, Howard University, 1978), pp. 150-160.

We are now at the hub of the issue. What is Christian conversion? I am convinced that the answer to this question is to be found by finding out what place the person gives Jesus in life itself. Let me explain. Persons conceive of a variety of powers which surround them, some are positive powers and some are negative, but all have some influence on people. This arrangement of the powers, as we understand them, is called cosmology. These cosmologies differ from person to person and from culture to culture. For example, in one culture, ancestral spirits are powerful; in another, the penal system established by the state, or the banking system is very powerful. These powers have direct bearing upon individuals in those societies. Now, what happens when Jesus enters these cosmologies? Does he simply take his place alongside the other powers? Does he confront any powers already there? These are crucially important questions.

A group of evangelical theologians from around the world met in Bermuda in 1978 under the auspices of the Lausanne Continuation Committee to debate this and other issues. They agreed on this statement:

> Jesus is Lord means more than that he is the Lord of the individual convert's world-view, standards, and relationships, and more even than that he is Lord of culture. It means that he is Lord of the powers, having been exalted by the Father to universal sovereignty, principalities and powers having been made subject to him (1 Peter 3:22). Conversion involves a power encounter.[2]

There can be no true conversion nor authentic discipleship which does not take seriously the fact that as Jesus confronted his world, so his followers will confront their

---

2. *The Willowbank Report—Gospel and Culture* (Wheaton, Ill., 1978), p. 21.

worlds. This confrontation takes place where the two kingdoms meet, the kingdom of God and the kingdom of darkness. When believers find themselves confronting the evil which surrounds them, they must take heart, for so it was with their Lord and Master, Jesus Christ of Nazareth.

Implications for Mission

1. Culture is not always a friend.

Christian fellowships live in a hostile world no matter where they are on earth. No culture, even if it claims to be Christian, is truly and consistently Christlike in all its parts. There will always be some antagonism between those whose allegiance is to Jesus Christ and those who live in a state of rebellion against him.

2. Christians are in the world but not of the world.

Christian fellowships should so participate in the living, dynamic presence of Christ that they interact with the world in exactly the same way Jesus did and as he continues to do today—with redeeming love. The community of faith is not an ark which is, when filled, taken out of the world as though the church exists for itself. It is a redemptive community which is in solidarity with all humankind, yet it judges the very world with which it expresses solidarity. It sees itself as part of the divine plan to bring all things into proper relationship with Jesus Christ.

6

THE CHURCH CONFRONTS

In the late 1950s the Kikuyu tribe in Kenya determined to use force to recover the land which the British colonial government had taken from them for the use of white settlers from Europe. The guerrillas' biggest obstacle was not the colonial government but the growing number of keen, revived Kikuyu Christians who refused to take up arms even though they, too, recognized the inequities in the way things were. So the "Mau Mau" organizers spent much of their energy trying to press these Christians into a united front. The result was that hundreds of the Kikuyu Christians died as martyrs rather than take up arms for either side. "What got into these people?" the tribal elders complained. "It is a disgrace to our tribe that we harbor those who are disloyal."

Something did "get into" them—the Spirit of the Lord—and they were changed from the inside out. Their traditional loyalties would have led them to fight but as Christians they had to forego use of violence. They did what they believed

Jesus Christ was asking them to do and they discovered that Jesus required something quite different from society. As they went about lovingly burying their dead, they realized that they were pilgrims and strangers on the earth.

Perhaps they remembered those words which Jesus spoke, "Blessed are you when men hate you, and when they exclude you and revile you.... Rejoice in that day, and leap for joy, for behold, your reward is great in heaven" (Luke 6:22-23); or "You will be hated by all for my name's sake" (Matthew 10:22).

The values of Jesus should become the values of his followers; these values conflict with the values of any age and culture. This is where the clash takes place. An apocryphal story tells how a person who was traveling with a surgeon discovered that his stomach was so ulcerated that he required another. Inasmuch as they were far from the hospital, the surgeon removed the stomach from a nearby goat and transplanted it in the fellow. After several months the man with the transplanted goat's stomach complained of having a ravenous appetite for hay and tin cans. This story rather crudely illustrates that if Jesus Christ changes our inner man, we will experience an inner compulsion to follow his value system rather than the fads and fancies of our age.

If a church is made up of true believers, it will ultimately come into conflict with some aspects of the culture in which it lives no matter where it is in the world, because no culture is a true friend of Christ. This is due to the very nature of the gospel as revealed in Jesus Christ. Therefore, even though signs of conversion and Christian growth will differ from one culture to another, there can be no hesitation in asserting that a church which does not confront its culture in some meaningful way is not really the church of Jesus Christ at all. It is simply another group within the local culture.

Take as an example the tribal bond, the oath, which binds the Kikuyu people together. There is something very beautiful about people caring for one another within the tribe. Jesus would certainly be for that. But when this value results in tribalism and all that follows from that, then Jesus' disciples rightfully protest, "We can go no further. Do with us what you must."

And what is true for Kikuyu Christians is true for Americans, Germans, or Chinese. Christian fellowships *are* different from this world. They have no option because Jesus is different from this world which is being ruled by Satan, the prince and power of the air (Ephesians 2:2). Christians are no less confrontational than Jesus Christ himself.

Confront What?

Each Christian fellowship must determine what aspects of their society they will confront. Normally they resist at those points where Satan is making the greatest inroads in their society at that particular time. Polygamy, for example, may be the demonic wedge in Tanzania while in North America materialism or militarism may be the issue. It is not appropriate for one church to tell another what it must confront even though openness to others in this matter is encouraged.

One of the primary reasons for the confrontational stance is that human greed and selfishness tend to foster exploitation. This is especially evident in economics and in political power. Given time and circumstances the few will wrest rights from the many in order to move toward some ideological utopianism or to consolidate some vested interest. These structures and systems are frighteningly open to demonic forces which further inflate and inspire the dehumanizing enterprises which evil people invent with amazing resourcefulness.

Jesus, the Creator and sustainer of the universe, expressed his profound disappointment with the way power, wealth, religiosity, self-righteousness, and just plain greed were ruining the beauty and the promise of that which he created. But he made clear that he would have none of this among his followers.

Jesus' warnings to the powerful still ring in our ears. Those empowered by wealth, like Zaccheus, he invited to repent; and those infatuated with their own self-endowed holiness, like the Pharisees, he challenged again and again to acknowledge their egocentric religious systems for what they were—simply a human way of avoiding responsibility to God and neighbor. Jesus saved his most shockingly picturesque language to describe those who should have known better, the scribes, the Pharisees, and the rulers of the temple, but who nevertheless went on their merry ways creating one rationalization after another. They were "whitened sepulchers," a "generation of vipers," "sons of the devil," and the like.

The world has not improved very much since AD 33. The battle may now be on a different field—our publicans and Pharisees are different, but the conflict is identical. People still seek power for their own advantage and by doing so they mutilate and maim the powerless. That in itself is bad enough, but the real cosmic consequences of sustained egocentricity or ethnocentricity is that it is absolutely contrary to the design and purpose of God, which is that all creatures should be moving toward unity.

In their social service activities and programs Christians are actually expressing their belief that all things should be unified in Christ. But full unification occurs when people believe in Jesus Christ and in turn involve themselves in loving, Christ-honoring service to all people. All selfishness and greed are diametrically opposed to the fulfillment of the purpose of creation which is that all creatures should love and be loved, should tend others and in turn be tended by others, should so participate in Christ that they will be forgiven of their sin and will have the grace to forgive those who harm them. All mission activity should be carried forward in the spirit of Jesus Christ, who is no respecter of persons, but views all men as of equal worth.

When the followers of Jesus confront the forces, institutions, and persons who are determined to preserve privilege above all else no matter what hurt they cause, they are fulfilling the will of him who stands among them, Jesus Christ the Alpha and the Omega. Any missiology which does not deal with human alienation which results from the fall will, of necessity, fail because that is humankind's basic problem.

Those who are enlightened and empowered by the Spirit of the Lord will not only confront evil by word of mouth, they will live confrontationally. But they will do so as servants and not as lords. They will exhibit in their own fellowships the reconciling nature of him who stands in their midst. This is essential. If, among the followers of Jesus, there are those who lord it over their fellows because of class, race, or sex, they are acting out of character with Jesus and that attitude must be exposed.

When the mother of James and John appealed to Jesus to have her sons sit one on his right, the other on his left, in the kingdom, Jesus rebuked her strongly in the hearing of the disciples:

> The kings of the Gentiles exercise lordship over them; and those in authority over them are called benefactors. But not so with you; rather let the greatest among you become as the youngest, and the leader as one who serves. Luke 22:25, 26.

Having noted that the church will confront the world, we should not be deceived into thinking that evil is only outside the fellowship and that everything inside is fine and dandy. If that were so there would be rationale for the church to separate itself from society and then pronounce doom on everyone else. Evil knows no boundaries. It will invade anywhere it is given half a chance to do so. It will even penetrate Christian fellowships. This does not mean, however, that fellowships should not speak up. They confront evil, not because they themselves are completely rid of it, but because evil is evil no matter where it shows up. There are not two Satans, one bothering the world and another bothering the church. He is one and the same and must be confronted whenever his deeds are manifest. This is such an important missiological issue that it warrants careful study.

The church may never be intimidated by those who insist that because the church is itself not entirely free from sin, it has no right to confront sin in the world. They insist that the church rid itself of all of the devil's works within its own brotherhood before they take on the world. Jesus' people have no regard for such niceties. Their struggle against sin is cosmic, beginning from right there where they are and from there to the ends of the earth. Who would ever be ready to enter mission activity if it was contingent upon being sent by a perfect sending community?

If the church is contextualized, that is, if it takes the realities of the local situation seriously, then it will be both in the world and yet not of it, just like Jesus was. If it would concentrate only on its uniqueness, it would separate itself as completely as possible from culture and world and therefore become irrelevant; on the other hand, were it to become completely accommodated, it would lose its saltiness and fail to have any meaning or substance at all. The danger is that we are always lured into following one or the other of these extremes. Normally, the church, after the first generation or so, falls prey to the pressures to accommodate itself to society. It then relaxes and convinces itself that the world is a friend to God.

Lesslie Newbigin, formerly a bishop in the Church of South India and now a teaching missiologist in Britain, has some harsh words for Western Christianity.

> How can the church become the bearer of that word of grace and judgment for the Western culture with which it has lived so long in almost total identification? . . . For centuries the churches in the West have seen themselves as the guardians and sustainers of the culture of which they have been a part. They have not—in general—seen themselves as the bearers of God's judgment upon this culture. If they had done so, they would have learned again that "challengingly relevance" means, in the end, suffering, and that suffering is the fundamental form of Christian witness.[3]

A contextualized church will speak so cogently against the works of the devil in its society that it will meet resistance just like Jesus. This is a fact as ancient as the church itself. Mennonite churches have sometimes tended to withdraw or move away rather than confront. But there can be no excuse for a non-confrontative gospel, for Jesus himself said,

> If the world hates you, know that it has hated me before it hated you. If you were of the world, the world would love its own; but because you are not of the world, but I chose you out of the world, therefore the world hates you. Remember the word that I said to you, "A servant is not greater than his master." If they persecuted me, they will persecute you (John 15:18-20).

---

3. Lesslie Newbigin, "Mission in the 1980's," *Occasional Bulletin*, Vol. 4, No. 4 (October 1980), p. 155.

It is hard to be more specific than that.

The church has no excuse to be a whit less confrontational than was Jesus Christ who was nailed to a cross of wood. Ultimately every Christian community, no matter where it is on our planet, will clash with some very significant aspects of the culture in which it lives. And it will suffer in the process. No culture on earth is a true friend to Jesus, not even our own.

Implications for Mission

1. Cultures contain good and evil elements.

While some aspects of all cultures are consistent with the spirit and teachings of the Lord and should, therefore, be preserved with great care, other aspects of culture are directly opposed to the gospel of Jesus Christ and, therefore, must be confronted.

2. Evil must be confronted.

Each fellowship or cluster of fellowships must determine the major and most harmful evils in their society and they must also determine how to confront these evil forces both within the fellowship and in the larger society. It is inappropriate for the church in one culture to insist that a church in another culture confront evil on the same fronts. The spirit of anti-Christ operates differently in different cultures.

3. The church fights spiritual battles.

Jesus Christ is not only the wisdom of God; he is also the power of God. His power is clearly evident in his ability to overcome the power of Satan and evil spirits. As Jesus himself confronted evil spirits in his ministry, so Christian fellowships confront them today. In the name of Christ they overcome the evil powers, albeit sometimes through suffering. Christians confront the evil powers as they are experienced in each cultural situation. In one culture Satan may work primarily through demonic activity and witchcraft, in another through the processes of secularism or materialism. In either or all cases the power of Jesus Christ over evil is available to overcome the evil spirits.

4. Each fellowship confronts evil locally.

Too often Christians fight battles which are not related to the ultimate spiritual battles in which Jesus is interested. The "fronts" of battle change constantly from culture to culture and from age to age. Each fellowship should discern what Jesus wants it to do and then do it, and should recognize the responsibility of other fellowships to determine the major battles in which they should engage. Each fellowship is engaged in a spiritual battle against the forces of Satan and, therefore, must take to itself the total provision available in Christ to wage a good battle which will ultimately be won when every enemy serves as a footstool for Jesus Christ.

5. Christians do not employ evil means.

The methods which a fellowship uses to confront society will be consistent with the teachings and the living presence of Jesus. Believers refuse to employ un-Christlike means to attain ends which they think are favorable to Christ.

7

THE MENNONITES,
IN OR OUT?

"We can either be a missionary church or a pure church, not both." These weighed words spoken in my hearing by a Mennonite layman several years ago highlight the problem facing Mennonite missiology. The underlying assumption is that we must choose to either be in the world or not of it. If we become a truly missionary church, some say, then we might as well give up the idea of even trying to preserve ourselves as a pure church.

Even though this might accurately describe how we see the problem, it also reveals that we think it is impossible to do what Jesus so clearly told us to do. And we know that that is not right. Are the two irreconcilable? Must we make a choice between being a mission church or a disciplined church? This question penetrates to the heart of the Mennonite missiological problem. A quick review of how we got into this frame of mind as a denomination will help us to chart the path ahead.

Anabaptist Beginnings

I base my apology for the existence of numerous denominations on the doctrine of the distribution of gifts (Ephesians 4). Denominations are inevitable because people want to feel a part of a group that they can actually relate to; that tendency need not be destructive but can, in fact, be quite constructive. Further, each denomination represents a particular way of looking into the Scripture. This is not to be deplored but should be seen as a way in which each makes a meaningful contribution to the total Christian church. Each denomination casts its crown (its history and hermeneutics) before the Lamb in humble adoration.

Initially the Anabaptists developed both a confrontationist stance and an evangelistic stance. Within the first three decades (1525-55) they were intensely evangelistic. Their rapid growth startled both the reformers and the Catholics. In due time they collided head-on with the powers which they discerned to be evil. They were both evangelistic and confrontational. The Anabaptist movement, as nearly as we can detect from the records, did a reasonable job of combining the dual mandate of being "in" the world yet not "of" it, somewhat like the New Testament church did. They had to make their own way as they went along, with no existing models to go by. So they did what they felt had to be done to be faithful to the Lord. They fashioned their own methodology, their own missiology, as they lived in obedience.

The Anabaptist religious awakening spread rapidly within the Germanic-speaking world in the sixteenth century but before the movement could break into either the Slavic, the Latin, or any other culture their evangelistic zeal subsided and the Anabaptist churches entered into "détente" with their neighbors. This was the price they paid simply to survive. Having begun as a movement which was both evangelistic and radical, they clashed with the powers that be; and when they were faced with the choice of either calming down a bit or extinction, they reluctantly chose the former. Yet they were radical. They solved the problem arising from their radical nature. Instead of primarily confronting the evils of society which did not go away, they concentrated on their own purity and life as a people of God. The Dutch Mennonites never faced this same excruciating moment of decision because they lived in a more congenial environment. They tended to accommodate themselves more to their national culture than the Germanic Mennonites. The Germanic Mennonites spun themselves a cultural cocoon whose basic strands were the themes and values of the German Anabaptists. Their communities differed radically as a whole from their "world," but they were confrontationists no longer. They confronted only those members who refused to abide by their standards. In this way they could be radical without being confrontationist.

Robert Ramseyer, a present-day Mennonite missionary, made the observation that "as a person with no heritage except the New Testament, [an Anabaptist] needed only to be concerned about the will of God as the new people of God understand it." He notes, however, that

> Such radical faithfulness is never possible for us in later generations regardless of the extent or depth of our faith. We recognize a faith and institutional heritage which has been handed down to us as coming from God and worthy of preservation. With this concern for preservation has come also a tendency to minimize separation from others, a tendency to play down the uniqueness of our faith and demonstrate that we also are good citizens playing a useful role in the world.[1]

---

1. Robert Ramseyer, "The Anabaptist Vision and Our World Mission," *Mission Focus*, Vol. 4, No. 4 (March 1976), Elkhart, Ind., p. 2.

We may wish to take exception to Ramseyer's thesis but he does make his point that religious movements are more confrontational in their early stages than later.

The Struggle Between Evangelism and Nurture

While it was more like a glowing ember than a raging fire, the evangelistic gospel survived in Anabaptist communities following 1570. It was never completely extinguished because of the Anabaptist's high view of conversion. But their theology focused much more on ecclesiology than on evangelism. They concentrated on perfecting the body, giving primary consideration to discipleship and "living the gospel."

Through it all, nevertheless, they stressed voluntary conversion, even of their own children, thus barely avoiding a culture Christianity in which membership is gained automatically by birth. How well they avoided the temptation to make Mennonites by birth is open to question because children born to Mennonite parents found it much more convenient and even preferable to accept the option to be Mennonites than to launch out and try to become productive members of the larger, secular society or to join other denominations. Nevertheless, evangelistic concern was strongly eclipsed by the strenuous ecclesiology which emphasized a pure church.

If we leap over three centuries—which is quite unfair—we can see the interplay of these two themes which the brotherhood did not integrate properly. But Mennonites could not enter mission with any enthusiasm until they did so. In 1865, the Mennonite magazine, *Herald of Truth*, the year after its founding, published an article on missions by Philip Moseman, son of a Mennonite bishop in Lancaster County in Pennsylvania. In this article Moseman affirmed those who were already giving to "aid the work of the Lord among the heathen." He noted that those who did so were doing it with the approval of their "dear ministers."[2] Then there was a long silence. No one dared cut the fuse which Moseman lit. The brotherhood weighed the potential upheaval if the denomination were to really become active in mission. How could the church be faithful to the command to evangelize and the command to be pure at one and the same time? The debate gained momentum in the church. Finally the debate broke out on the pages of the *Herald of Truth*.

Editor Funk set forth a possible solution to the problem by suggesting that the church should "not only teach and instruct her own children or members, but the world—all men, of all nations, tongues, colors, and conditions."[3] The "nations" were to be taught the "all things" as perceived by the Mennonites. The "all things" really had to do with reinforcing the concepts of radical nonconformity to the spirit of the age and nonresistance in all relationships, even before enemies. For the Mennonites these were self-evident truths which should be embraced by all Christians. They felt called by God's special providential act to hold these twin doctrines high amid apostate Christendom.

In 1882 Funk had moved so far along this line that he was then discussing the propriety of building bridges with American society for the sake of evangelism. He tied the Great Commission and Mennonite understandings of the church together. "We are to live in one another's society," he wrote, "so that we may . . . be a help to each other, and . . . glorify God together. This is what the church of Christ

2. Theron F. Schlabach, *Gospel Versus Gospel* (Scottdale, Pa.: Herald Press, 1980), p. 35.

3. *Ibid.*, p. 36.

is.... [We are] not to keep these teachings to ourselves only. God designs all men to be saved ... everywhere."[4]

The *Herald* slowly picked up both the mission theme and the "pure church" theme. But if Mennonite historian Theron Schlabach's analysis is correct, no satisfactory formula was devised to bridge this theological gap. He notes that at the turn of the century

> No longer was th~ *very content of salvation* to be found in ...
> discipleship.... Now salvation became a matter of the
> Reformers' preoccupation with guilt of past sin, a revival-style
> acknowledgement of that sin, and a turning to a Christ who
> had fulfilled the ritual of sacrifice to a judging God.[5]

Schlabach probably makes the case too strong because Anabaptist themes did persist to a large extent even as the denomination was embarking on mission. But it is true that this was done without a satisfactory missiology which combined Christology with ecclesiology. Yet who of us works out our theology completely before we do something? It is usually the other way around. We obey and then we struggle with the implications of that obedience. In this way Mennonites are not unlike Peter in the house of Cornelius when he admitted he had not yet thought through all of the implications of his being there. The fact that there was additional work to be done is picturesquely put by Schlabach:

> ... at century's end Mennonite Church people were not com-
> pletely in step [with Protestant missions].... The new for-
> mula brought Mennonites close to the missionary movement,
> where they could hear the band play and unconsciously move
> with its beat. Still, they moved stiffly, cautiously, and a bit
> aloof.[6]

---

4. *Ibid.*, p. 37.
5. *Ibid.*, p. 51.
6. *Ibid.*, p. 53.

The Style of Mennonite Missions

It was certainly true that the modern missions movement had its own mystique, its own methodology, its own self-image, and its own ethos. Wilbert Shenk, a Mennonite missions administrator, has listed a number of these problems, not the least of which was the concept of comity which designated geographic areas to different denominations.[7] Mennonites had learned how to survive among the maze of denominations in North America and Europe, but they were not prepared to be the dominant denomination in any geographical area. They had originally rejected this approach as Constantinian but as they entered modern missions they found themselves falling into step with other mission agencies. It was not easy for them to baptize by the hundreds in their "territory" because they were conditioned by history to think of themselves as a remnant people among "worldly" churches.

Our style and, to a large extent, our theology of mission were borrowed from those who had gone before us into mission, particularly the "faith" missions. But "Saul's armor" was a better fit than one might have guessed at first. The various Mennonite bodies (including Brethren in Christ) have been quite successful in transcultural mission both in numerical and other terms.

Through the efforts of the major Mennonite boards, there are now Mennonite fellowships in forty-one nations and there are Mennonite-sponsored programs in more than seventy nations. Each day, on the average, about eighty persons come to Christ through Mennonite evangelism, over half of whom become active members of local Mennonite fellowships. Mennonites plant a new church every thirty-six

---

7. *Mission Focus*, Vol. 5, No. 1, Elkhart, Ind. 1978.

hours. There are now 650,000 Mennonites in the world, two thirds of whom are Westerners. By AD 2,000 there will be over a million Mennonites, at least half of whom will be from the so-called Third World.

It is estimated that Mennonite giving for mission and service exceeds twenty-five million dollars a year or roughly sixty dollars per member. Add to this the many man and woman hours put into emergency and relief services and the total is quite significant.

Mennonites have taken up the missionary challenge with unbelievable enthusiasm. On a per capita basis they have contributed much to world mission, certainly more than many denominations of similar size.

There was nothing unique in the way the Mennonites went about mission. This is rather startling because they did have a distinctive theology. But they failed to develop an evangelistic methodology which was consistent with their kingdom theology

Mennonite Kingdom Theology and Mission

One of the dominant theological images in the Mennonite Church is the concept of two kingdoms on earth, one ruled by God and the other by Satan. This two-kingdom theology has served the brotherhood well, but it also militated against the development of a comprehension missiology. This is such a pivotal issue that we must go into it.

One of the images which Jesus often used to describe the effects of his ministry was the "kingdom." This was not the only concept he employed, but he did use it again and again to communicate to his disciples the essence of his work among people. He spoke of the kingdom as a living, growing community of people who are inspired by a value system which conforms to the mind of Christ. This kingdom stands over against the kingdom of Satan. The two owe allegiance to different kings; they live by two different motifs, one nurturing life which culminates in eternal life, the other fostering death which ends in eternal death.

The backdrop for this theology is a military scenario with two opposing armies locked in combat. As each king tries to overcome the other, the battle goes forward. This battle takes place in the spiritual world but its effect is felt among the living; in fact, the living participate in the same cosmic conflict (Revelation 12).

This two-kingdom theology influenced Mennonites profoundly; they have struggled with its implications for centuries. Robert Friedmann, in his helpful book, *The Theology of Anabaptism*, (Scottdale, Pa.: Herald Press) claims that two-kingdom theology undergirds all Anabaptist-Mennonite thought. James Juhnke chose for the title of his history of General Conference Mennonites in Kansas, *A People of Two Kingdoms* (Newton, Kan.: Faith and Life Press). Mennonites are drawn irresistably to the two-kingdom theme like moths to a light. The Hutterites and Amish have taken this two-kingdom world-view so far that they have actually translated that theology into sociological forms—separatistic communities. This thinking is engraved, to some extent, on all Anabaptist self-understandings.

For centuries this theme dominated Anabaptist-Mennonite theology. It became the foundation stone on which their doctrines of nonresistance and nonconformity were based. If Christians are in one kingdom and non-Christians in another, went the argument, then the styles of these two worlds must be different, their loyalties are to different "kings," their values are different, and their methods of conflict resolution are therefore different. Jesus told Peter emphatically that if his kingdom were of this world, then they should use the methodology of this world; but if his kingdom were not of this world, then his followers should not fight like everyone else (John 18:36).

Mennonite communities reinforced this two-kingdom awareness by employing a multitude of symbols like dress codes, greetings, architecture, and shibboleths. Their life rituals, including education and mutual aid, were carried out in accordance with their theological stance which emphasized nonconformity and nonresistance. When it came to the matter of being both in the world but not of it, they concentrated particularly on the latter. As a result, Mennonites developed a highly sophisticated confrontationist stance which, by the beginning of the twentieth century, characterized the brotherhood. They were, in the standards of the age, highly "peculiar people." They had managed to cast their confrontationist stance in concrete cultural forms. They were the "plain" people in a fancy world.

The two-kingdom notion, as earlier noted, is burnt into our thinking as a people. It is probably the essential motif which forms our self-understanding. In fact, if a Mennonite fellowship anywhere in the world fails to see itself as separate and distinct from the kingdoms of this world, that fellowship is viewed as somewhat apostate.

This affects our views on baptism. In the Mennonite tradition the Mennonite view of confrontation or radicalness is inherent in our understanding of conversion and expresses itself in water baptism. We believe that when responsible adults turn from their sins to serve the living God, they experience conversion or the new birth. Water baptism expresses and seals this radical change. It also symbolizes the radical nature of the Christian church because the supplicant submits to the authority and discipline of the community of believers who bind and loose in the name of

Christ. The two-kingdom theology has, therefore, served us much better as a way to understand church than to understand evangelism. Said another way, it clarified how much we were not "of" this world but it did not help very much in giving guidance about how to be "in" the world. And that is one reason why we have failed to develop an adequate missiology.

From AD 1525 onward affiliation with an Anabaptist fellowship required a very radical understanding of the Christian faith. In fact, in the early decades (1525-1545) it often meant imminent danger from the authorities, both civil and religious, to the extent that the movement produced hundreds of martyrs in northern Europe. Mennonites have always honored the martyrs. One item in a typical Mennonite household is the *Martyrs Mirror* (Herald Press), a large volume which chronicles the stories of hundreds of martyrs. The martyr imagery, even today, continues to galvanize the faith of Mennonites because the martyrs are persons who have demonstrated that they have turned their eyes toward Christ and that by so doing they have rejected this world and its allure. Martyrs are essentially confrontationist, and that in its purest human form.

These two concepts, the confronting kingdoms and the courageous martyrs, touch a resonating string in Mennonite people everywhere. We are indeed a people who see ourselves in conflict with our "age." We have really majored in this department so that we have a much clearer notion of who we are not than who we are. These concepts must now be expanded to include the mission mandate. Our obedience to the Lord's command to go into all the world and make disciples has moved us to a point where we must pause and get our theology up-to-date.

Need for a New Image

Mennonites stand with an evangelistic mandate in one hand and a mandate to stay pure and undefiled from the world in the other. The tensions which result from these two imperatives are sometimes quite intolerable. We have already seen churches split because these two mandates could not be reconciled. It is at this point where narrowly viewed two-kingdom theology is inadequate. The two mandates are like the twins, Jacob and Esau, who while children of common parents, could not live in peace together.

This is such a pity because both are essential aspects of the gospel of Jesus Christ. I believe that the two can be held with authenticity if there is a new imagery, a new understanding of reality which gathers up both aspects of the gospel in an integrated way. What might that new reality be and how can it be envisioned? This is the task before us.

Implications for Mission

1. The church has a dual mandate.

Every fellowship should be involved in evangelism and nurture. These two aspects of the gospel must go hand in hand and should not be allowed to increase tension within the fellowship. One way of avoiding the tension is to regularly update theology which takes into account the totality of experience and knowledge.

2. Christians witness in word and deed.

In Jesus Christ there is no conflict between evangelizing by word or by deed for they are two expressions of redemption. Christian fellowships should refuse to polarize on the issues of evangelism and nurture, or of a "spiritual" ministry versus a "physical" ministry. All contribute directly to the fulfillment of God's redemptive action through Christ.

8

GOD AMONG HIS PEOPLE

The Necessity of a Biblical Base for Missions

For some people it may not seem appropriate or necessary to write a theology of mission; to them there is simply no doubt that Jesus meant what he said when he gave the Great Commission to "make disciples of all nations" (Matthew 28:19). I agree that we should "get up and do it." Time is running out, but the question remains: How should we go about it and what are our goals? One marksman always had a perfect score. He managed that by shooting first and drawing in the target later. Sometimes we are in danger of this temptation. We need to consider the target carefully. Our mission should grow out of an understanding of the major themes of redemption history as recorded in the Scriptures, an understanding of our own "redemption history," and the relevant facts of our time.

As long as the Mennonite denomination was small, slow-growing, and homogeneous, it was not necessary to work at this, but the situation has changed. Now we are a rapidly growing, truly multicultural fellowship of believers spread over more than forty nations, with people from even more ethnic groups than that. It is appropriate that at this time in our pilgrimage we grasp the nettle. What is our theology of mission? How can we reconcile the dual mandate to evangelize the world and to keep the church pure? How can we be in the world yet not of it?

Two basic questions cry out for answers. First, how does Jesus Christ relate to human history? And second, how is he forwarding his purposes among us? There is only one place to turn for answers to these questions—the Bible. The Scriptures trace how God revealed himself through Jesus Christ and they describe his place and ministry in the world today. By entering into the very life of the Bible we can align ourselves more meaningfully with the activity of God as he deals in love with humankind.

The Old Testament—Forming a Covenant People

The first chapters of Genesis set the stage for redemption history. We may raise our eyebrows a bit as we read how the awesome Creator God relaxed among his creatures and even enjoyed being with people. He was "at home" in the universe that he created. But one species among the creatures, humankind, became so inflated with their own importance that they said "no" to what they knew was God's command. By doing this humans set themselves against God and effectively alienated themselves from God. The result was predictable; God, seeing he was unwelcome did not push himself on humankind but gently tried to win them back to himself.

God went about this wooing process in a number of ways but primarily through dealing with human conscience. That little voice speaking within people kept reminding them that it is really better to obey God. He also spoke through nature itself which was a more or less constant reminder of human-kind's dependency on forces outside their own control. Then on special occasions God appeared through direct and in-direct revelations such as with Abraham and others. But people experienced the divine presence only intermittently at best. It was as though humankind had built a wall of such massive thickness between itself and God that any meaning-ful, close relationship between God and people was unthinkable.

In the course of redemption history God provided a way for a chosen group, Israel, to escape captivity in Egypt in hopes of forming them into a new people. It was for this reason that he brought them to the foot of Mt. Sinai in Arabia where he established his covenant with them and then sealed the covenant by actually taking up residence among them. One is reminded of the earlier state of affairs when God did move freely among people.

This interaction between God and his people was sym-bolized in that remarkable tent-building, the Hebrew tabernacle. The tabernacle symbolized not only a new hope, but it gave the Jews a new way of thinking about reality. The major feature of the tabernacle was a simple, but quite remarkable revelation of the fact that the Creator God wanted to dwell as a living presence among his people.

God Revealed Through the Tabernacle

The primary object of the tabernacle was to announce that God had chosen a community of faith which was invited to enter covenant with him and with one another. By so doing, they are given access to the presence of Yahweh himself who inspires, enlightens, empowers, cleanses, enables, equips, and leads his people to participate with him in the process of reconciling a fractured world.

A "thumb nail theology" of the Hebrew tabernacle is: God is among his covenant people in a very special way. God is fully there to meet their total needs in every circumstance. The fact that he chooses to live in the midst of his people even though they are impossibly "stiff-necked" is a recurrent theme of Hebrew theology (Exodus 33 and 34). This God presence is what makes Hebrew theology unique and from this belief flows a theology of community which constitutes the heart of the theology of missions.

The tabernacle was a shadow of what is real. But in Jesus Christ and his church the imagery becomes reality, the shadow becomes substance, the life and light himself fulfills in a most remarkable way that which was so clearly represented in the tabernacle. As Paul put it in referring to Jewish festivals, new moons, and sabbath, "These are only a shadow of what is to come; but the substance belongs to Christ" (Colossians 2:17).

However, before looking at God's full revelation in Jesus Christ we will pause to explore the imagery of the tabernacle because we see in that remarkable symbol some of the major themes of the gospel. These themes are good building blocks for laying a foundation for a theology of missions.

After the patriarchal era, Israel was formed as a people, separated out from others via their exodus from Egypt. They were welded into a socio-religious community as they moved slowly through the wilderness of Arabia. One experience after another taught them that the cohesive factor in their life as a people was the presence of Yahweh. They had a common ethnicity, but that in itself was not the source of their peoplehood. Yahweh declared time and again that without his presence there would be no meaningful "Israel." It was this tabernacle which symbolized that fact. After it was built he moved in! In Exodus we read, "So Moses finished the work. Then the cloud covered the tent of meeting, and the glory of the Lord filled the tabernacle.... (Exodus 40:33, 34, 38). God spoke out of this cloud of his glory. Once again he was resident on the earth in a particular place.

Clustered around the God-presence stood the furniture of the tabernacle—the altar, the lampstand, the shewbread, and much more. As the worshipers pondered this building, they were made keenly aware of the fact that God was placing himself squarely in the context of human needs, hopes, and aspirations.

Human-divine history is a grave tale of increasing alienation. First man rejected God, then human alienation followed as a matter of course. And even nature assumed a hostile relationship with humankind. The tabernacle announced that God intended to reconcile these three; God, man, and nature. There is a way for people to live at peace with God. God is prepared to meet all of their needs. This is beautifully symbolized in the tabernacle and its ancillary services. The tabernacle points to the church and the church symbolizes and even participates in the culmination of the age when all things will acknowledge the lordship of Christ.

We now turn our attention to the tabernacle's themes.

God chooses to take up his residence among his people even though they are rebellious and self-seeking (or maybe because they are rebellious). He took the initiative to reestablish his presence among people. It was not that some clever people built an attractive tabernacle in order to lure a reluctant God into a place near them. Many religions are built on that assumption. Rather, God determined to take up his residence among humankind, not because they sought him but because he sought them. God always takes the initiative.

a. God desires a covenant relationship with humans.

This is an amazing aspect of the redeeming God. He actually invites sinful people to enter covenant with him in such a way that he involves himself intimately with their problems and destiny. The relationship is conditional upon their submission to God's revealed will, of course.

There must be agreement between the parties in a covenant relationship. But people are very weak and they tend to grow weary of carrying their end of the covenant commitment. The promise, however, is there continually. It is not surprising that people desert God. What is profoundly moving, however, is to realize that God actually wants to have a covenant relationship with sinful, struggling people.

b. Sin must be cleansed.

Not just anyone can rush into Yahweh's presence. He is too holy for that. For that reason Aaronic priesthood was established. Through ritual cleansings and so forth, at least one person could stand before God, the high priest. He was God's channel of grace and forgiveness. In effect all had equal access to God because all could participate in the priestly system.

c. He is a self-revealing God.

God's presence was not there in the tabernacle simply to lend an aura of mystery to an otherwise common tent or as an authenticating halo around the Israeli throne. Rather, he was there in order to instruct, to listen, and to communicate with his creation in a very special way.

> There I will meet with the people of Israel. . . . And I will dwell among the people of Israel, and will be their God. And they shall know that I am the Lord their God, who brought them forth out of the land of Egypt that I might dwell among them; I am the Lord their God. Exodus 29:43 ff.

> Let them make me a sanctuary, that I may dwell in their midst. Exodus 25:8.

Moses was undoubtedly astounded when he met God in the tabernacle.

> And when Moses went into the tent of meeting to speak with the Lord, he heard the voice speaking to him from above the mercy seat that was upon the ark of the testimony, from between the two cherubim; and it spoke to him. Numbers 7:89.

The creation motif is reinforced here. In the creating process God spoke in a way which revealed his will. God is a holy God and is, in a way, unapproachable. He therefore secretes himself to a certain extent, yet not so much so that he removes himself from humankind. In fact, the whole tabernacle apparatus is in reality a housing for the divine presence, not to make him remote, but to provide a way to bring him close, even closer than one would dare hope possible.

d. He is for the people.

God keeps coming down because that is where the people are. He enters their sinful society and through his presence instructs, cleanses, and renews the people so that they can participate with him in the work of bringing all things into unity under himself, beginning, of course, with the covenant community. He concerns himself with their problems. He leads them to places where their welfare will be enhanced and he enlightens them on the way. He participates in their history, sheds light upon their peoplehood, and inspires them to go on in faith. In some deeply mysterious way God's welfare is linked to the welfare of his people so he struggles with them. He is one of them, yet "wholly other." He is with them in their counsels, not as an observer only but as a participant—in fact, as the major participant. It is to the tabernacle that the people of God retreated when they wanted more light, wisdom, and power. In the tabernacle they could communicate directly with the presence. Furthermore, the covenant community was a complete universe because God dwelt there. All of the resources of God were at hand for any present or future eventuality.

e. He is concerned about the totality of human need.

The sacrificial system promised the absolution of sin and guilt. Conflict resolution was provided in the priestly services. Enlightenment and understanding as symbolized by the lampstand was promised. And real bread representing the physical aspects of life held a prominent position near the altar.

God takes personal as well as communal needs very seriously. All areas of life are sacred in God's presence and every area of life is affirmed by the Creator God.

f. He is a pilgrim God, moving toward a predetermined goal.

It is difficult to imagine a people making a more radical social adjustment than the Israelites made when they moved from the established, highly sophisticated, Egyptian culture to tribal cultures in Canaan. God committed himself to pass through these changes with his people. The Shekinah glory which was cloud by day and fire by night was a symbol of movement. The covenant people are "on the move." They know God, but only in part. They continue their journey into a deeper understanding of God.

g. He is for the nations.

While the tabernacle containing the presence stood among the Israelites, its purpose was to so inspire and lead Israel that they could be light to the nations. This required a constant turning outward in order to take the light of the God presence to all the world. Israel did not do this very well at all. Albeit, God willed that through Israel's actions all nations might come to the light.

h. He is the God of hope.

The fact is that God's presence graced the tabernacle and in turn the nation of Israel aroused hope in other nations, because it revealed clearly that God cares and he desires to be the all-meaningful presence for humankind. The tabernacle was temporary; the God presence was eternal. The eschatological aspects of the presence were not at all clear, but certainly a God who cared so much that he entered into human experience in the tabernacle provided a focus for hope, not only for the present but also for the future, and not only for Israel but for "the nations."

i. He is the God of law and grace, of judgment and of mercy.

God has standards for people. He is an ethical God. The Ten Commandments are commands which describe the nature of the moral laws undergirding the universe. They are not just some ideal toward which Israel is to move. On the other hand he is the God of grace symbolized by the sacrificial system which provides for atonement. This counterbalance of law and grace enables a society to operate with a clear definition of rights and obligations, but it also provides a way of forgiveness through the process of restitution. It assumes the fallibility of man and makes provision for the fact. It makes a way for the strong and for the weak.

j. He is the God of the past and the future.

The tabernacle includes historical symbols such as Aaron's rod to remind the community of God's past benefits which serves to shape faith. It also includes symbols of hope such as the mobile Shekinah, the bread and the light, all reminders of God's provision for the future.

The tabernacle complex is so full of stimulating symbolism that it is rather difficult to lift out the most meaningful symbols. Every generation in every culture can see in that amazing cluster of symbols known as the Hebrew tabernacle a wealth of images to ponder.

Post-Tabernacle Decline

One might well ask, what went wrong? It is remarkable that the tabernacle, which was such a powerful demonstration of renewed divine-human reconciliation, did not produce the kind of people for which it was prepared. When the Israelites entered Canaan, they were distracted by a thousand distractions and the tabernacle fell into disuse, at least as God intended that it should be used.

From Tabernacle to Temple

David, the king, knew in his spirit that God should have a dwelling place on earth and he set about to locate some of the original tabernacle pieces, but it was left to his son Solomon, the son of peace, to actually build the magnificent temple which was baically a sophisticated tabernacle. When it was dedicated to God the people renewed their covenant and "the glory of the Lord filled the temple. And the priests could not enter the house of the Lord, because the glory of the Lord filled the Lord's house" (2 Chronicles 7:1, 2)

But Israel soon forgot all about that covenant or at least so it appeared. The temple became more a sign of national pride than anything else; and so it was little wonder that the people began to go about building other national institutions with little regard for the presence of God.

Israel began at Sinai as a theocracy in which the God presence was the pivotal point. In the passage of time the kings of Israel replaced the Shekinah, the royal court eclipsed the tabernacle. Israel became a sedentary people rather than a pilgrim people open for new ventures in redemption. Instead of God owning Israel, Israel tried to own God. Slowly they underwent a metamorphosis which changed them from pilgrims to settlers.

From Temple to Exile

Then Jerusalem, with its court and temple, were destroyed and the Jews were taken into captivity where they lamented what had happened, but they could not understand why. God sent them prophets such as Ezekiel to explain what had gone wrong—that they had broken their covenant relationship with God. Ezekiel comforted the brokenhearted Jews by telling them that they could worship God just as well in Babylon where they were captives as in Jerusalem with its once mighty temple. All they needed to do was repent. Jeremiah taught that the remnant should remain true, wherever that remnant is found and, furthermore, that Israel is not for itself but is part of God's plan for the redemption of the world. These were lofty sentiments which the people failed to comprehend.

The inter-testamental period was a time of theological confusion. The Jews had long since lost the pilgrim aspects of their tabernacle period. They had also tried to rebuild their holy sites, the temple included, only to be conquered by a succession of nations and finally Rome. The Jews longed for the return of the Shekinah glory, God's presence.

It is little wonder that sects developed which sought him through mysticism and other esoteric ways.

The futility of it all was underlined by Herod who, in order to gain political advantage, built the Jews a temple for their God to live in! From the human point of view, it looked like the idea of God reestablishing his presence among his people was doomed. They had once again driven him out by their persistent disobedience and rebellion.

Implications for Mission

1. The church is God's dwelling.

The church is not simply an interest group or a task force with a job to be done. The church is nothing less than God's residence on earth. The church is now supposed to do what Israel the nation failed to do, to be light for the nations. Christian worship concentrates on the presence of Christ among the believers and both announces and celebrates the fact.

2. Fellowship is essential.

Missions will encourage those persons who have responded to the love of God through Christ as Savior and Lord to cluster into authentic fellowships which acknowledge and live by Christ's presence. Even though persons are converted one by one, each one responsible before God, a fuller expression of the gospel is demonstrated in the local fellowships of believers which is the visible expression of the body of Christ.

3. Provision is made for whole persons.

God wants to meet the total needs of people: their minds, souls, and bodies. No part of a person is less redeemable than another. In Christ all of humankind's needs are met. As the body of Christ, the church will minister to people in their totality. It is not very helpful to determine the primacy of any particular need. All need is met in Christ.

9

CHRIST AMONG HIS PEOPLE

Jesus Is the Hub

After a North American churchman had visited some newer churches overseas he remarked, "It is a miracle that these churches hang together at all because they are full of new believers. The fact that they continue to function is living proof that God is at work!" He was saying more than he knew. His experience of church had been in old, traditional settings where customs and procedures were established, where the people knew one another, in fact where the congregations were communities. The people were all members of the same "tribe" and to a certain extent depended on one another for fellowship and even for mutual support. It was not only a spiritual community but a sociological one as well.

The newer churches usually lack the sociological "glue" to bind them together. They are often a conglomerate of persons from a variety of families and social classes. In addition, some members are marginal people in their own communities. The mix in some of the newer churches is strikingly dissimilar to the solid, old churches made up of respected noncontroversial people who have a rich heritage of congregational life.

Maybe that is the reason the newer churches are much more aware of their dependence upon the living presence of Jesus, just to survive as fellowships! Older churches might survive at least for a while on their tradition and sociology; not so the newer churches. Without Jesus in their midst they would not have much of a chance.

But this is precisely what we should expect of the gospel. Jesus promises to live among the fellowships, and the people in these clusters can be as diverse as you care to imagine. The thing that sets the church apart from all other groups is that Jesus is there. It is as simple, yet as profound, as that.

We pick up the theme of God's presence in the Old Testament. They knew how much God wanted to be among them, but they were also keenly aware of the fact that their persistent disobedience kept God at bay because he was, after all, the judge, and they were sinners. The remarkable tabernacle and the sacrificial system pointed to something better, but they could not understand what that might be. They even had trouble trying to figure out what the Messiah idea was all about. But God revealed his plan; it was that he would meet all man's need in the coming Messiah, Jesus Christ. Jesus would come to earth, not as a visitor passing through, but he would come with the goal of actually establishing residency here.

The Temple Is Political

The inspired writers pick up the tabernacle imagery. John wrote, "The Word became flesh and dwelt [tabernacled] among us" (John 1:14). The tabernacle image is significant because Jesus taught in the shadow of the magnificant temple, which was the outgrowth of the Hebrew tabernacle. It occupied 26 acres of land, built by Herod, a most impressive structure indeed. It was a brand-new edifice and it looked like it was to be there forever. That temple was the very apex of the Jewish God-concept; Herod built God a fixed dwelling on a rock which could not be moved. Its inner sanctuaries were reserved for male Jews only and God. Instead of being the God of Hebrews, Yahweh became the Hebrews' God, a domesticated version of the dynamic, moving God of the pilgrim people's tabernacle.

Some of Jesus' most bitter invectives were reserved for the chief priests of his time who were appointed to be the guardians of the temple. Their job was to keep the people sanctified so that God could dwell among his people with at least a modicum of comfort. However, rather than periodically purifying the temple of corruption, they were actually gaining profit from the corrupt commerce which went on precisely where God almighty wanted to dwell. I once heard an African brother say, "God is a gentleman and will not go where he is not invited." Is it possible that "two penny" money changers could drive the maker of the universe out of his temple? That is precisely what happened.

While the chief priests were getting gain from what went on in the temple, the scribes and Pharisees were embellishing the law. Both were using the blessings of God for their own self-centered ends and they expected God to respond to their every whim like a puppet on strings. It is clear that God sincerely desired to dwell among his people, but it was impossible for him to live with any effectiveness at all among people whose every thought, plan, and dream was diametrically opposed to his intentions. So Jesus confronted the chief priests and the scribes.

Jesus tried to make this as clear as he could during his week of passion. Matthew 21 records how Jesus cleansed the temple, particularly that part set aside for Gentile worshipers. It was turned into a place where Jews brought and sold their sacrificial animals and probably other merchandise. The temple, like the fruitless fig tree, aroused expectation which was not fulfilled. Matthew recorded how Jesus reminded the chief priests that they did not repent under the preaching of John the Baptist, nor did they bear fruit, and that tax collectors and harlots have a better chance of getting into heaven than they. God expected the fruits of righteousness to come from the temple as he expected figs from the tree and there was none; instead of justice there was oppression. He had blessed the Jews so that they could be a light to the Gentiles, but they were corrupt to the core. The temple must be replaced by something greater. These were hard sayings but they tell what the plan was and what went wrong. God wants to live among his people, but they drive him out. When this happens he must leave; he has no option.

Stephen, the martyr, also alluded to what the Jews did to both the temple and the law. In effect he told them that they failed God miserably, that they were irresponsible caretakers of both temple and law, and that Jesus is above both temple and law. Stephen got stoned for his trouble; he was the first Christian martyr.

Jesus Makes the Temple Unnecessary

When Jesus began to minister, he did so with little reference to the temple in Jerusalem except that he had gone there at age twelve and confounded the priests with his insights. The Samaritan woman, aware of the Jews' fixation on Jerusalem, asked Jesus, the Jew, where to worship, implying that one should worship where the God presence is. Jesus told her, a Samaritan who respected neither temple nor law, that "The hour is coming, and now is, when the true worshipers will worship the Father in spirit and truth" (John 4:23). God is not confined to the temple, Jesus implied. But God still wants to dwell among his people. The temple served no other purpose than as an illustrated lecture of God's real intent which is to dwell among his purchased community. In itself the temple is nothing—it is not only dispensable but undesirable. Jesus was uncompromising in his view of the temple. Its destruction in AD 70 had nothing at all to do with whether there was a place for God on earth or not. By then the Jews were already conceding that their future was not dependent upon God dwelling in a building. Of course, Jesus had said as much many times over.

Returning to Jesus' life, he patiently revealed the startling good news to his disciples that he must die and then rise from the dead after which he will take up residence among people in a new way. "Where two or three are gathered in my name," he announced, "there am I in the midst of them" (Matthew 18:20). As he was among his disciples in the flesh, so he promised to be with them in the Spirit following his resurrection and ascension.

Jesus Announces His Intentions

The disciples caught little glimpses of God's plan. While on the mountain of transfiguration they saw the Shekinah glory, the God presence, fall on Jesus. Does this presage, they may have asked, the return of the Shekinah to dwell among the people? Jesus told them that he must die, that he must go away. He told them of the comforter, the Holy Spirit, who was to come. They could barely conceive of that but it was at least a comforting idea. Little did they realize that Jesus Christ of Nazareth, after his ascension, would actually live among them just like he had done in the past—in the Spirit, however, not in the body.

He told them in his week of passion, "If a man loves me, he will keep my word, and my Father will love him, and we will come to him and make our home with him" (John 14:23). Is it possible that this could be true? He fulfilled the ancient prophecy of Zechariah, "Sing and rejoice, O daughter of Zion; for lo, I come and I will dwell in the midst of you, says the Lord" (Zechariah 2:10).

One of the images which Jesus employed to describe the new way was the "kingdom." He told his followers that it is the "Father's good pleasure to give you the kingdom" (Luke 12:32). This kingdom requires the existence of a king, one who reigns, not through normal kingly might, but by the power of a poured out, sacrificial life. In this new kingdom people are reconciled to God and to each other. They share a common life under the authority of their common Lord. This kingdom is already here even though it is imperfect.

Jesus continues today to relate to his disciples like he did on the night of the first day of resurrection. "On the evening of that day, the first day of the week, the doors being shut where the disciples were . . . Jesus came and stood among them and said to them, 'Peace be with you.' When he had said this, he showed them his hands and his side. Then the disciples were glad when they saw the Lord" (John 20:19-20).

His promise to them was secure, "I am with you always, to the close of the age" (Matthew 28:20). Jesus is not an absent Lord; on the contrary he graces the fellowships of love with his life-giving presence. The original disciples exalted in this miracle and so have believers ever since.

The apostles who witnessed this daily miracle of divine

grace, who enjoyed the enthusing presence of Jesus Christ among his followers, pondered how this happens and why. It is this theology of the living presence of Jesus (Christology) which is so carefully spelled out in the apostolic writings.

Implications for Mission

1. The church is where Jesus dwells.

The church exists where the followers of Jesus Christ meet in his presence and where they submit their individual and corporate lives to his lordship. In the fellowship of believers all live equidistant to Christ. It is only their own sin which separates them from him and from one another. Believers are enabled to live in peace with one another because through the blood of Christ, which represents his poured out life, they are cleansed daily as they repent of their sinfulness. If the church becomes just another interest group in society, it is thwarting rather than helping the purposes of God to make the good news of salvation known to all people.

2. Fellowships are equal before God.

The fullness of Christ is available for each fellowship on earth regardless of the environmental or sociological conditions. All fellowships, therefore, are equally close to Christ and it is prideful for any fellowships to boast that it has a preferential position with Christ. The concepts of "daughter churches" and "younger churches" must be tempered by the realization that there is only one kind of fellowship, a group of persons with Jesus in their midst.

3. Each fellowship is responsible for world mission.

Each fellowship is in reality a center for world mission. No fellowship which clusters around Jesus Christ, and which places itself under the authority of Scripture, can escape its missionary mandate.

10

CHRIST IN THE
NEW TESTAMENT CHURCH

From the Temple to the Body

While he was in the body Jesus could be only one place at any time. But after his ascension it was possible for him to be spiritually present everywhere all of the time. This boggles our imaginations but it is true. Because of this fact, he can live in every fellowship. This must have amazed the early Christians. Could the God of glory whom the heaven of heavens (2 Corinthians 6:18) could not contain be present in the new, often seriously deficient, Christian fellowships around the Mediterranean shores?

I am sure another question crossed their minds, particularly the Jewish believers. Will the Shekinah glory move from Herod's temple (if it in fact was ever there at all) to their little house meetings? He promised to be where his followers clustered. But did that mean that he was going to desert the temple? Or could it be that he wants to inhabit both the Jewish temple and the newly formed assemblies?

Or is it possible that his true presence will remain in the temple and that those who believe in the Messiah must join themselves with the temple? We know that the disciples worshiped in the temple after the ascension (Acts 3). Jesus did not hesitate to refer to Herod's temple, which had been completed while Jesus was but a boy in Nazareth, as His Father's house. So in some mysterious way God did inhabit that temple.

Pentecost changed all that. Ten days after Jesus ascended, one hundred and twenty believers gathered for prayer in Jerusalem within the vicinity of the magnificent temple. They were startled when flames or tongues of fire appeared in their gathering reminiscent of the presence of God's glory in the tabernacle and the temple. This was God's dramatic announcement that when Christians gather, he is there in a special way. His presence moved to where they were. He shifted his point of reference from the temple to the believers, the newly forming body of Christ.

The effect of this must have been stunning. Had the church now become the apple of God's eye instead of the Jewish nation with its magnificent temple? At one and the same time this delighted the believers but the responsibility was awesome. It was up to them to take the good news to every land so that God's spirit could fill the earth. And this is precisely what happened. Where believers gathered in Jesus' name, that same divine presence was among them. In fact the presence of the Holy Spirit became the basis of the fellowship of believers.

The Body of Christ in Ephesus

This all sounds a bit fanciful and idealistic and perhaps a wee bit spooky. We find it difficult in our rational Western culture to concede that where believers gather, Jesus is in fact there through the work of the Holy Spirit. But this is at the heart of the whole issue. If Jesus is not present with us in our fellowships and assemblies, then what dynamic does the church have that is unique from the other interest groups in the world? Are our fellowships simply social clubs or are they the place where God almighty dwells?

The story of what occurred when the good news invaded Ephesus will help us to understand the nature of Christ's body, the church. We travel through time to visit the fellowships in Ephesus in AD 68, two years before the Roman legions demolished Herod's temple in Jerusalem.

How the gospel first entered Ephesus is not known, but it probably was first heard in the town's synagogues where Jews worshiped. A few people believed within the synagogue community and a small Hebrew Christian fellowship emerged.

When Paul entered Ephesus on his second missionary journey (Acts 19), he found believers within the Jewish community. An evangelist, Apollos, sent by the thriving church of Alexandria in Egypt, had already been there and many were convinced to believe as a result of his ministry. Prominent among the local Jewish believers were Priscilla and Aquila, wife and husband, who had recently been expelled from Rome because of rising anti-Semitic feelings there.

When Paul arrived he joined with the local believers in their evangelistic efforts. He concentrated his energies on the synagogue community from which a few believers had come to faith in Christ. But after three months he decided to move into the mainstream of Ephesian Gentile culture because the nonbelieving Jews became obstinate. He was able to hire a downtown lecture hall during the heat of the day from Tyrannus, a Hellenist teacher of philosophy whose students probably had a "siesta" during that hour. This shift placed Paul in the center of Ephesian life, a culture which was dominated by occult practices and the worship of the fertility goddess, Diana.

Many people believed in Christ and they were added to the few Jews who had already believed. The Christian fellowships were, therefore, made up of people of mixed background. In fact, there were three distinct cultures in the Ephesian fellowships.

There were, first of all, the "pure" Jews, the "Ben David's" and the "Ben Isaac's" so to speak. They were Christian, all right, but they continued to hold to the hallowed and highly respected Jewish symbols like circumcision and the kosher eating taboos. Apollos of Alexandria, referred to earlier, itinerated throughout the church, including the fellowships in Ephesus, encouraging not only Jewish Christians to continue to obey Old Testament law, but he insisted that the Gentile Christians must also submit to the Old Testament law in its entirety. Quite a few of the Christians believed this was the right approach and they tried to press their views on everyone.

Second, there were the proselyted Jews, the "converts," those with "pagan" genealogies who attached themselves to the synagogues but who sometimes felt that the pure Jews discriminated against them. Many of these "marginal" Jews found the Christian faith attractive.

Then, third, there were Gentile Christians who were baptized into the Christian faith without first being circumcised. Many of them never did submit themselves to circumcision and, therefore, they bore the brunt of Jewish criticism. They were also an easy target for the Christian Judaizers like Apollos.

Imagine the strains and the stresses in those fellowships. They were all Christians but they had little else in common.

These groups made up the fellowships to whom Paul wrote the Ephesian letter, probably from prison in Rome, about 12 to 15 years after the fellowships were begun.

Paul experienced in Ephesus what he witnessed everywhere else. When the disciples of Jesus assembled, the spirit of the Lord was there. As God's glory filled the tabernacle and then Solomon's temple, so he filled the little fellowships with his glory. Those fellowships became the new tabernacles, the new temples on earth.

Paul does not hesitate to make the far-reaching assertion that the church is God's dwelling place. His words still amaze us. "So then" he wrote, "you are no longer strangers and sojourners, but you are fellow citizens with the saints and members of the household of God, built upon the foundation of the apostles and prophets, Christ Jesus himself being the cornerstone, in whom the whole structure is joined together and grows into a holy temple in the Lord; in whom you also are built into it for a *dwelling place of God* in the Spirit" (Ephesians 2:19-22, underlining added). Paul is not just using fanciful language to get a point across, he is stating a fact; God inhabits the church in a way in which he inhabits no other place on earth.

That is what makes the Christian fellowships so unique. It was not simply a group of people with similar interests like the society of Ephesian sophists, nor was it a secret society like the Gnostics whose unity grew out of initiation ritual and participation in certain mysterious rites. The church is unique because it is the place where God chooses to live. It is unique because of him, not because of the disciples; the disciples are, in fact, quite ordinary people.

New Testament Christians experienced the living presence of the Lord in their fellowships. This is clear from all of the sources. The Holy Spirit enlightened their understanding so that they could experience Christ.

But what difference did the presence of the Holy Trinity make in the fellowships? What direction was God moving his people in their pilgrimage? The church in Ephesus elucidates this beautifully.

In this extraordinary pastoral letter Paul addressed all of the groups with a single profound statement which had to do with their life together. It is startling in its implications. Paul states:

> He [God] has made known to us in all wisdom and insight the mystery of his will, according to his purpose which he set forth in Christ as a plan for the fulness of time, to unite all things in him, things in heaven and things on earth. Ephesians 1:9, 10.

This was already beginning to happen where the divine plan was taking shape in which diverse believers were being brought together into fellowships of love. This is not how messianic Jews thought it was going to be according to their reading of the Scriptures. They envisioned a strong king who would reestablish the throne of David and then rule all humankind and bring peace through the reestablishment of the law. What a contrast! God is working out his plan, not in imperial courts or on the battlefield but in the little Christ-centered meetings of believers just like those in Ephesus whose only point of commonality was their love for Jesus. The fellowship of believers is where the course of history is turned around to face toward Jesus Christ. Said another way, the fellowship is the setting in which the cosmic drama is being enacted. It is, in its truth, "heaven on earth."

Paul is not using metaphorical or platonic imagery to describe the church. In platonic philosophy that which is seen is but a shadow of the real thing. In that case the church would be but a symbol of reality and not reality itself. Contrary to that idea, the Christian fellowship is not the shadow of heavenly reality, but the church partakes of the very essence of the reality of Jesus Christ because the fellowship, the church, is nothing less than his very body, with him as the head (Ephesians 4:15, 16). The Ephesian Christians were not simply reflecting history, they were making it. They were creating something new and marvelous on the earth. The church matters.

To human eyes one of the frailest things in the universe is the Christian fellowship, especially where it includes culturally diverse peoples as in Ephesus. Normally you would not bet on the survival of such fellowships but survive they do, weathering unbelievable storms. And they had better do so because if the fellowships fail there is nothing to take their place in God's plan. As modern parlance puts it, the fellowship is "where it's at."

In writing to the Ephesians, Paul's description of the place of the Christian fellowship in the cosmic drama fairly soars. One would think he is describing the fantastic temple of Diana whose 137 sixty-foot-high marble pillars dominated the Ephesian metropolis. It was four times the size of the Parthenon in Athens. It had a permanence and a grace which inspired the poets. But Paul is not describing that highly organized, wealthy religious enterprise; what he is addressing is the little struggling Christian fellowship tucked in the shadows of that colossus. What is new on the earth? These loving fellowships which clustered around the living presence of Jesus Christ. The temple of Diana was destroyed long ago but the church now covers the earth.

The fellowship of believers, Paul proclaims, is not an afterthought in the mind of God, a good idea which came to him when all else had failed to work. The fellowship of believers was the ultimate goal of God in all of his preparatory work from the foundation of the world (Ephesians 3:11). It is

God's way of beginning to restore the effective unity of all things; it is to be done under Jesus in the fellowships.

Paul wrote,

> When you read this you can perceive my insight into the mystery of Christ, which was not made known to the sons of men in other generations as it has now been revealed to his holy apostles and prophets by the Spirit; that is, how the Gentiles are fellow heirs, members of the same body, and partakers of the promise in Christ Jesus through the gospel. To me . . . was given . . . to make all men see what is the plan of the mystery hidden for ages in God . . . that through the church the manifold wisdom of God might now be made known to the principalities and powers in the heavenly places. Ephesians 3.

He then went to great pains to explain that this is made possible because of the death and resurrection of Christ. Jesus crucified, he explained, is like a door or a passage, similar to the rent veil of the temple. Jesus' sacrificial atonement opens a way so that anyone may enter in. People enter through grace, not through merit; when into Christ they continue to live by grace. Both Jews and Gentiles pass through or into the crucified Christ where the enmity between them ceases. Then as new creatures in a new fellowship, Jews and Gentiles live in love which gives the lie to Satan and the "principalities and powers" who convinced the world through the ages that this is impossible. Jesus resides in the fellowships and as his disciples make him their Lord, they experience a Christo-centric unity which supersedes all man-made unities.

The major cultural gap in the fellowship at Ephesus was that between Jews and Gentiles. They belonged to antagonistic cultures which hated one another with age-old hatred. The Jews absolutely despised the Gentiles and the

Gentiles in turn viewed the Jews as proud, conceited exploiters. But this antagonism provided the very context in which the power of Jesus Christ was to be most visibly demonstrated. In fact, I believe that if the love of Jesus had failed to bring Hebrew and Greek together in Christ, then all else would have been phony, including claims of salvation itself. If salvation does not contribute to the reunification of all things, beginning with the alienations in the fellowships, it is by definition faulty. When, therefore, a Jew in the name of Christ embraced a Gentile in a little fellowship in Ephesus, it was an event of cosmic significance. The principalities and powers saw and were either shocked or overjoyed, depending on whether they were with Christ or against him. (Ephesians 3:10).

Even though the Jew-Gentile antagonism was the one which plagued the church most, other conflict situations existed in that society which also needed healing, including the persistent battle of the sexes. Husbands were lording it over their wives and wives were resenting it. Paul told them both to take the way of Calvary, which meant wives will submit to their husbands and that husbands will love their wives as they do their own selves. In Jesus husband and wife are brought together in unity, the same way Jews and Gentiles are reconciled. Paul also pointed to the intergenerational friction within the fellowships. Hostility persisted between fathers and sons. He instructed the young to obey their parents and the parents to be careful lest they provoke the children. Parents and children relate to one another in the presence of Jesus. This is also true of the fourth area of alienation in Ephesian society, that between labor and management. It all sounds so modern. He reminded the slaves that they were to obey their masters and he reminded the masters that they also have a Master in the Spirit and that they should learn from him how to rule. Persistent tension areas such as these can dissolve into loving relationships in Christian fellowships.

Where such reconciliation is not happening in a fellowship, either Jesus is not being given his place "above every name" or the fellowship is just a mimicry of the true spiritual fellowship and is not Christianity at all. Where the Spirit of the Lord is and where that Spirit is given sovereignty human barriers will dissolve and, like the apostle, the believers will know no one "after the flesh." Love replaces hate, judgment gives place to grace. This miracle occurs because Jesus Christ of Nazareth resides in the fellowships. It is not a human achievement but is the result of the abundant grace which flows from the Lord.

Paul said that the church is where "the manifold [many sided] wisdom of God might now be made known" (Ephesians 3:10). Time and again Paul comes back to this point: the most convincing manifestation of the presence of the Lord in the fellowship is unity. This is not incidental. It is crucial to the destiny of humankind and all the universe.

All Things Reunited in Christ

All things will be brought together under Christ. The writer of the Hebrews noted, "Now in putting everything in subjection to him, he left nothing outside his control. As it is, we do not yet see everything in subjection to him" (Hebrews 2:8). This is because of the rebellious nature of humankind. But surely in the church the believers are repenting of their rebelliousness and are living in an open relationship with not only the Lord but with one another. This is the style of the coming age when everything named will acknowledge that Jesus is who he claimed he is, the door, the light, the only begotten Son. His will is already being done in the fellowships as it is done in heaven.

This means that the fellowships of believers are the darlings of heaven because what happens in them sets the course for man's destiny. This is of such strategic importance that the Father, Son, and Holy Spirit—the triune God—provide resources to the fellowships of believers around the world. Each fellowship, each Christian now has available "the fullness of God" (Ephesians 3:19). The windows of heaven are opened and the gifts necessary for the reunification of all things pour out into the amazed and amazing fellowships around the world.

We all well know that the church is not quarantined against internal friction and hostility. They owe their uniqueness not to the fact that they are perfect, but to the fact that Jesus Christ is among them to judge hostility and to cleanse hostile feelings as his followers acknowledge their sinfulness and pride and as they repent of these social poisons. It is in their worship that the Christians are reminded of the fact that before God they are all sinners needing daily grace. They are not saved by the works of their hands or the hands of their fathers; they are saved by the gracious act of redemption

Peacemaking begins in Christian fellowships. If the fellowships are riddled with strife and antagonisms, and if they have given up the struggle for unity, what do they have to say to a divided world? It is amazing how vitriolic one section of the brotherhood can become toward another. Paul asked the question, "Is Christ divided?" Denominational pride can take on these dimensions and often does. This is to be deplored. Jesus Christ, whom we acknowledge to be the center of our fellowships, does not encourage such destructive activity. Christ, by the way, does not withdraw from the fellowships because of their pride and stiff-neckedness; he suffers, pleads, and prays for their unity (John 17:20, 21).

The grand vision, the plan of God, is meant to be experienced in actual living fellowships. The believers to whom Paul wrote lived in the heavenlies, in Christ, but they were also in fellowship in multicultural, bustling cities like Ephesus. The fellowship is the mission of God at work and it is the work of the mission of God. It is the way of mission and it is the result of mission.

Jesus Christ in the midst of his obedient people is the means and the end of the missions as it is the means and the end of the plan of God now revealed.

Implications for Mission

1. Peace centers in Jesus Christ.

Peacemaking begins in the local fellowships from which it overflows into the not-yet-believing world. Peace results not primarily from a philosophical or a catechetical teaching or conviction, but from the presence of Jesus Christ in whom all things will ultimately find their wholeness.

2. Christian unity supersedes human differences.

As local fellowships experience Christ's unifying presence, they will testify to a bond of peace in love which transcends denominational and other barriers. Unity arises from the reality of Jesus' presence and is not based upon cultural homogeneity, or any other human classification. Those fellowships and people who testify to the living presence of Christ in their midst are uniquely related to one another even though they may differ in their expressions of faith.

3. The Church is central in the redemptive plan.

Christ is resident among the believers as the first sign of the eventual coming together of all things. God is bringing into being a model of the new humanity which is unique upon the face of the earth and even, for that matter, in heaven.

It is possible for the world to see clearly the nature of the eschatological age by observing fellowships in action today, for the redemptive presence of Christ gathers and also scatters the believers in loving ministry and witness.

4. Humanistic utopias are doomed.

There is no place for utopianism in the Christian faith—the unbelieving world is not reforming itself or even repenting. It continues to vent its violence at will and evil people seem to emerge in even the most benevolent enterprises showing that persons cannot transform themselves. Yet Christians are glad when people anywhere attempt to live by the values of love, peace, nonviolence, mutual aid, and justice. The fact that those virtues are not extinguished in the nations clearly indicates that God has not abandoned them.

Every bit of shalom, wherever it is, should be acknowledged as ultimately coming from God because in some way it contributes to the coming together of all things in Christ. But shalom does not save, Jesus Christ does.

11

CHRIST
IN THE HEAVENLIES

Our final biblical study takes us to the book of Revelation, the major apocalyptic writing in the New Testament. Its language and imagery are strangely different from the other, more ordinary, writings of the New Testament. The Revelation reminds us of certain portions of Daniel and Ezekiel, full of fascinating creatures doing amazing things. John in this Revelation reports a vision which abounds with symbols and images which were probably more "revealing" to the original readers than they are to us today; however, we can grasp the central features of this remarkable book. Its message is that as God was present in the tabernacle and temple, Christ is now present throughout the world where believers gather. We turn to this great book.

John, the Revelator, was caught in the paradoxes of his era. The evangelizing church had finally collided with emperor worship. Before that the church's main persecutors were the irate Jews. Now, however, to be a Christian was interpreted as being disloyal to the emperor. Faithfulness to the message of peace and love took its toll as hundreds of harmless Christians fell under the hand of violent governmental authority. John himself felt the strong arm of the empire when he was exiled to the island of Patmos. Within John's mind a conflict raged. There on the island he faced a new set of problems. Things were not going at all well. It must have looked to John as though Jesus had abandoned his throne on earth. Maybe it was different in heaven. John needed to be assured of this. God in his mercy supplied this new vision.

As the curtain lifts in chapter 1, John saw the temple's holy places. He realized, certainly, that the physical temple was now a heap of rubble, having been destroyed twenty years before during the rule of Vespasian. He noted that lampstands were in place in his vision, along with other furniture, and in the center of it all walked the high priest tirelessly tending to his high priestly tasks. John realized at once that this was Jesus moving with love among the fellowships. He was the all mighty one (golden breast plate), the all wise one (white hair), the all seeing one (eyes like flaming fire), the all knowing one (the ancient of days). Furthermore he, not Satan, had the keys to death and hades. This vision was, at first, almost too much for John; he fell down as though dead, but when he saw its significance he rejoiced.

The second major pictorial revelation is recorded in chapters four and five. The God of all might sits on the rainbow throne surrounded by worshiping creatures. He holds a scroll which no one can open. A search is mounted in the heavenlies to find someone worthy to open the book. They eventually discovered the only one who was worthy, the Lion of the tribe of Judah; he could do it.

He appeared from the midst of the throne and the elders.

It was, again, none other than Jesus Christ of Nazareth, now appearing as a lamb slain. He took the scroll and broke its seals. He wanted John to see the full revelation of God in the written book. John stood amazed as this seemingly mild, nonviolent lamb performed a feat of strength which had defeated all others.

All heaven sang the new song,

> Worthy art thou to take the scroll
> and to open its seals,
> for thou wast slain and by thy blood
> didst ransom men for God
> from every tribe and tongue and
> people and nation,
> and hast made them a kingdom and
> priests to our God,
> and they shall reign on earth.
> Revelation 5:9, 10.

Jesus Christ of Nazareth is the prince of glory. He is at the right hand of the Father. He dispenses gifts to the church (Ephesians 4). This is the Jesus who delights in taking up residence in Christian fellowships. It is not necessary for him to leave heaven to do this because he is omnipresent; while he graces a little fellowship on earth, for example, he continues his residence at the Father's side. Jesus, therefore, joins heaven and earth together in a loving bond of unity.

We can learn many lessons from the Revelation which concern the activity of Jesus Christ today. We will pick up only a few of the many meaningful aspects of Jesus' present ministry to the saints in the world, particularly those that have to do with missions.

Jesus Christ Is Central

The most striking feature of the heavenly vision was the

delightful centrality of the person of Jesus Christ. All the action revolves around him. He is the center of attention, the precious one among many. He stands ministering "in the midst of the lampstands" (1:13). The pascal lamb was first seen "among the elders" (5:6). And, "the Lamb in the midst of the throne will be their shepherd" (7:17). This refrain is repeated again and again in the heavenly imagery; Jesus Christ is the center of attention. As he is forever heaven's joy, he is eternally "in the midst" of his covenant people. Revelation reiterates this central tenet of the Scriptures and does so in a most winsome and convincing manner.

Jesus Identifies with His People

Second, Jesus does not stand off to the side but lives "in the midst" of his people, identifying with them, and sharing their lives with them. He tends their lampstands, so to speak. Jesus Christ is a living presence now active in the fellowships (congregations) of people who love and adore him (1:13ff.). His followers live according to his desire. His disciples are described as those who follow the Lamb everywhere he goes (7:17). Jesus Christ lives among his people.

Jesus Leads His People

Third, Jesus instructs, protects, inspires, and leads (7:15ff.) his people. He does this by actually associating with them. But he does not displace the Scriptures; the place of the Scriptures is secure. Each fellowship of believers has as its resource the Scriptures, the presence of Jesus, and the Holy Spirit who quickens the Word and brings its light to bear upon the problems facing the fellowships. Each fellowship is, to a degree, a hermeneutical or discerning community.

The reason the Scriptures are life-giving is because Jesus stands in the Scriptures as he stands among the believers, "in the midst." Certainly the Scriptures in their entirety authenticate Jesus but even more important, Jesus authenticates the Scriptures. We read the Scriptures through the eyes of Jesus because he is the one through whom all the Scriptures make sense.

He continues the gracious ministry which he began with the two who were walking forlornly to Emmaus, "Beginning at Moses and all the prophets, he expounded unto them in all the scriptures the things concerning himself" (Lk. 24:27, KJV). The Scriptures are true because Jesus is the truth and not the other way around. Christians who cluster in the name and power of Jesus Christ constantly submit themselves to the mind and will of Jesus as they read the Scriptures. He alone can open the "Book."

I am not despising higher criticism of the Bible even though some people make a case for that. Truth is truth and Christians should not fear truth. But we must never forget that the truth became flesh and blood and its name is Jesus Christ (John 1:14). Jesus would remain truth even though every creature were to pronounce him false. The Bible is true because Jesus is the truth. Christians love their Bibles; they memorize Scriptures and ponder them day and night. But without Jesus Christ there is no eternal life. The Scriptures do not save; Jesus Christ saves. Jesus challenged the Pharisees saying, "You search the scriptures, because you think that in them you have eternal life" (John 5:39); but they missed the point of the Scriptures, which is explicitly and beyond contest that Jesus Christ is the only one through whom eternal life is available.

Having said this I hasten to add that the Scriptures are not for "private interpretation." Peter was emphatic on this: "First of all," he wrote, "you must understand this, that no prophecy of scripture is a matter of one's own interpretation, because no prophecy ever came by the impulse of man, but men moved by the Holy Spirit spoke from God" (2 Peter 1:20, 21).

Each fellowship of believers comes to the Scriptures directly and each fellowship is enabled by the Holy Spirit to interpret the Scriptures, but each fellowship must remember that it is a part of the total historical body and is not an isolated entity responsible only to itself. Each fellowship, therefore, interprets the Scriptures in light of the totality of the learnings of the total church. Of course, those learnings are not available to each fellowship, but at least the point must be made that fellowships should interpret the Scriptures on the basis of the fact that their group is part of the broad hermeneutical community. This does not, however, relieve them of the responsibility of submitting themselves to the disciplines of biblical interpretation. It simply means that the "prophecy" which they discover or discern must be submitted to other fellowships for processing. So even though each fellowship is enabled by the ministry of the Holy Spirit to approach the Scriptures directly in order to discover the mind of Christ, all learnings can and should be tempered by the theologies of others. This is one good reason for denominational connections.

Jesus Draws All Persons to Himself

The church is not made on earth, it is made in heaven. It supersedes all human relationships because there Jesus Christ is acknowledged by all, and he is the center of the new community of faith. The church is the place where every tongue, tribe, and nation will find a place which is congenial and where active sharing occurs. Each group brings its riches to Christ and within the body the resources are shared. This is the hallmark of the fellowships—their active love for one another, which is symbolized by their desire to make their resources available to all. This was the case in the early church and the Revelation brings this into clear focus as all types of people cluster around Christ like the spokes surround a hub.

All Creatures Will Acknowledge the Lordship of Christ

Finally, the totality of the plan of God for all creatures is that they should be united in Jesus Christ (5:13ff.). The fellowships of believers are the first places on earth where God's creatures actively participate as a prototype or, better yet, as the first models of the eschatological destiny of all creatures.

The reason unification can take place is because there is an answer to that which destroyed unity in the first place, the problem of sin, which is simply a word to describe rebellion against the will of the Creator. The will of God is not something which God decided to impose on unwilling creatures simply as a method to establish his authority or in order to show who is in control. The will of God is the life-giving, creative principle which upholds the universe, both spiritual and material. It is the "given" of the universe like the nervous system is a "given" in a human body. The will of God is a description of the way creatures can be creative and life-affirming. When this essential principle is rejected and an alternate way is sought, things go wrong. When the cosmos is disrupted chaos results and instead of unity, peace, and creativity there is hostility, alienation, and destruction.

The Scriptures as well as human history describe humankind's tendency to rebel against the Creator; this is the one constant in the human experience. We are quite resourceful in creating structures, laws, and all kinds of institutions to reduce the destructiveness of our deep alienation from God, neighbor, nature, and even ourselves. But we discover that even as we create our towers of unity, we fall into confusion and disunity. The universe was meant to cohere around God and nothing can take his place.

So the basic issue is man's alienation from God. If this problem is not dealt with, then the universe will struggle with itself. There is only one way to put it all right and that is to get a remedy for this rebellious spirit which insists on telling God, "But we have another way." There is no other way. There is only one way, Jesus Christ of Nazareth, God in the flesh, who exposed the horrifying nature of humanity by allowing persons to put to death the Creator. But you say, they did not know he was the Creator. How else could he have presented himself? He was not disguised. He said openly, "I and my Father are one. If you have seen me you have seen the Father." Jesus was not God in disguise; he was God revealed but human beings resist that idea with anger.

But Jesus did not remain in the tomb. He sprang back to life and ascended to heaven where he appeared to John as the paschal lamb, the perfect sacrifice once offered for all time. His poured-out life, his blood, absorbs hostility thus perfecting atonement so that man can stand before God and, in joy, say "yes" to him.

The essential factor in the bringing together of all things in Christ is the blood of Christ which symbolizes the entire Jesus event—his life, death, resurrection, ascension, and present ministry among the fellowships. His broken body is where alienation ceases, it is the occasion for warring enemies to throw down their weapons and discover that in Jesus they can love one another.

This is why Jesus appears in the Revelation as the paschal lamb. It is because of his work of atonement that people from all nations, tribes, and tongues can join in the harmony of all things. John experienced it as a song, "Worthy is the Lamb." This is precisely what happens on earth. People respond to the love of Jesus and cast their sin on him. He forgives sin and makes it possible for sinners to forgive one another. As alienation is removed by this cleansing, a new creation, a new cluster of creativity is produced, which astounds the world. Former enemies now love one another with the atoning and reconciling love of Jesus Christ.

Mission is the bringing together of all things in Christ. This is God's mission and the fellowships not only demonstrate what that mission is but they themselves become the means whereby God's mission is carried forward.

Now and again I've made allusions to the hope that all creatures, including nature itself, will once again be at peace with God and humanity. The Scripture is not very explicit on this point but one thing is clear, human rebellion somehow upset nature's harmony with God. Therefore when humankind is reconciled to God, the way is opened for nature to once again align itself with God. A second point is clear: the unification of all things definitely includes the natural world. Paul said that all nature groans for redemption (Romans 8:22). African people often asked about the place of animals in heaven. I had never thought much about that. But if alienation is removed, then humans and nature should have a shared destiny.

Christians have a different attitude toward nature than unbelievers. They try to work in harmony with nature because nature lives by the same divine principle as humanity. They refuse to exploit nature to the extent that its productivity is curtailed. They also believe that all humankind should have adequate access to earth's resources. Christians see the care of nature as mission because it is part of bringing all things together in Christ.

Returning to our original thesis, we do not believe that people are redeemed and then left to live their lives as best they can. We believe that even though people are saved as individuals, they live as fellowships which are graced by the presence of the living Lord. As the lamb is the center of heaven, the one to whom the new song is sung, so he is the center of fellowships of believers on earth. His gift of forgiveness is perpetually employed in these fellowships. John described it in these words, "If we walk in the light, as he is in the light, we have fellowship with one another, and the blood of Jesus his Son cleanses us from all sin" (1 John 1:7).

The Book of the Revelation is not only a vision of what is to come; it is the announcement, from God's viewpoint, of what actually is. And no one can frustrate the final outcome even though from our vantage point it might look like the plan of God is suffering significant setbacks. God is working to bring all things together in Jesus Christ. This process is going forward. "We do not yet see everything in subjection to him. But we see Jesus (Hebrews 2:8, 9a).

Implications for Mission

1. The church shares in mutuality.

As members of a local fellowship share life with one another, so fellowships themselves share with one another although their gifts and resources may differ. Some have considerable resources in monetary form, some are strong in the area of spiritual vitality, or in the ability to suffer, for example. The way of Jesus is to so blend resources that the will of Christ can function in the spirit of unity.

We entrust resources to Christ who stands among us. If giver and receiver acknowledge Jesus as Lord and Savior, there is no need to fear. As servants of Jesus we serve others, but in reality we glorify Jesus Christ by participating with him.

2. *All cultures have a witness.*

God is interested in his total creation and the movement of history is toward the ultimate consummation of all things in Christ. God has not left himself without witness (Acts 14:17). The knowledge of God is residual in all peoples. Furthermore, he is actively engaged preparing all people for the full revelation of himself in the person of Jesus Christ. Some cultures are more open to Christ than others, but in no culture is God totally absent. There are illustrations within each culture by which Christ can be comprehended. Missionaries should seek for those illustrations (paradigms of grace) and employ them in evangelistic communications.

3. *The church witnesses in and to the state.*

The church always lives in tension with the powers; it is called to witness, to be leaven, a light, a conscience. All world systems participate to some degree in evil, yet totalitarian governments seem to be the worst because they tend to isolate themselves from the witness of the church. They often become tragically demonic.

Although it is often difficult for the redeemed community to know how to give its witness to the state, the church as a worldwide fellowship must creatively find the way together to witness against injustice, the violations of human rights, and other forms of evil perpetuated by the state. Sometimes that witness can only be given by the local or national fellowship; at other times it requires the wider community of faith. In the matter of church-state relationships, the missionary needs to be especially sensitive to the counsel of the brotherhood within which he serves. As both a guest and a member of the local fellowship, the missionary must affirm that fellowship in its hour of crisis.

4. *The gospel judges selfish exploiters.*

Living in Christ implies identifying with God's creation in all its forms. Christ's followers are involved in bringing creation into unity with him. They judge all alienation. There is no place in the plan of God for human beings to exploit one another or to plunder or pollute their planet. They are not owners or possessors but are called to be faithful stewards of all the good gifts of God. There must be bread for all people.

5. *Believers become communities of the Spirit.*

The Holy Spirit is among the believers to enlighten their understanding of Jesus Christ and to distribute his gracious gift.

The Spirit makes the Lord Jesus present and real. He guides the believers into all truth as he quickens the Word. He comforts and convicts them and prompts them to do what Jesus desires. The fellowships live "pneumatically," filled with the Spirit individually and corporately (1 Corinthians 3:16; 6:19).

12

A MISSIOLOGY
FOR OUR TIME

The Goal of Mission

This study raised two major questions. First, what is the mission of God? Or restated, what is God's purpose? And, second, what is God's way of carrying out that mission? In summary, the mission of God is to bring all things under Christ, to establish unity among his creatures so that they can participate in the redemption of all creation. It is toward this goal that God's people move. His people are those who have already responded to the call of Jesus Christ and who fellowship in his presence, enlightened by the Scriptures and led by the Holy Spirit.

The question then arises, how should the church conduct itself and how does it relate to a world which is, as yet, not believing? Does it preach the word, feed the hungry, or what? Is the church for the world or is it against it? Does the church confront the age or does it accommodate itself to the age?

Pursuing the Goal

The answer to these questions, as anticipated, is to be found in the glorious fact that Jesus Christ, our risen Savior and Lord, inhabits the fellowships of believers and there he guides the disciples to do his will. We can ask each other, "But what should we do?" The answer is simply, "Keep Jesus central and so live in him that he can tell us what to do." Jesus cares deeply and he will make his will known.

The late dean of Mennonite missiologists, J. D. Graber, said it well.

> When these basic functions [word and deed] of the church, the body of Christ on the earth, become separated and lose touch with each other, the church needs to be reminded of this Christological unity. When these two basic functions become separated and out of touch with each other, the cause lies in the fact that the church has lost her vital relationship with Christ, the head of the body.[1]

Graber concludes correctly; it is not a matter of whether we are doing too much of this or too little of that but whether we are in a vital relationship with Christ. I am taking this one step further by attempting to clarify the nature of our relationship with Christ. It is explicitly stated in Scriptures and joyfully attested to by Christians through the ages that Jesus Christ of Nazareth resides in his fullness in the fellowship of believers. He is that close and he means to make himself totally available. And he is there to create hostility-free communities of love which join him in the glorious task of bringing all things together under him.

So the sum of the whole matter can be resolved in what goes on in the fellowships and in their relationship with the

---

1. J. D. Graber, *The Church Apostolic* (Scottdale, Pa.: Herald Press, 1960), p. 53.

world. It is impossible to even imagine a New Testament theology which omits the church. So missiology is really Christocentric ecclesiology, to use Greek words; or in more humble terms, God is working out his plan of redemption through fellowships of believers who cluster around Jesus, their Lord.

Anabaptist Precedents

The Anabaptist renewal is exhibit "A" if we are looking for examples of fellowships which acknowledged the crucial importance of the Holy Spirit in the fellowship. The Schleitheim Confession affirms the Holy Spirit "who is sent from the Father to all believers for their strength and comfort and for their perseverance in all tribulation until the end."[2]

Menno Simons wrote,

> We believe and confess the Holy Ghost to be a true, real, or personal Holy Ghost, and that in a divine way—even as the Father is a true Father, and the Son a true Son; which Holy Ghost is a mystery to all mankind, incomprehensible, inexpressible, and indescribable . . . divine with His divine attributes, going forth from the Father through the being of the Father and the Son."[3]

All of this sounds ponderously theological and does not adequately describe the way the brethren lived life in the Spirit. They were constantly breaking new ground and, therefore, relied heavily on the daily activity of the Holy Spirit. That they elevated the Scriptures to a lofty position is irrefutable but they never made the Scriptures the fourth person of the Trinity. The Scripture was of a different quality than the active presence of the triune God in their fellowships. Their fellowships were essentially spiritual or

---

2. Erland Walter, "Holy Spirit," *The Mennonite Encyclopedia*, Vol. II, p. 795.
3. *Ibid.*

pneumatic fellowships. Their testimonies reveal their delight in Christ which resulted from a fresh understanding of the fullness of Christ made available to all believers, great or small. Their life together was less credal than it was spiritual, less conceptual than experiential, if these two aspects of faith can be distinguished. They were so enthused about the presence of Jesus that they were prepared to die for him.

This spiritual union created a bond between the brethren which superseded all family or natural ties. They did not cluster around a new religious idea or, as some have claimed, around a political ideal which led to the peasants' revolt, but they clustered around Jesus Christ just like the early church did and they sought to live his life in European society. Having no precedents to follow, they had to rely heavily upon their common experience of Christ. They did not set about to confront their age; that simply happened because their age was out of tune with what they understood the will of Christ to be. Nor did they develop theologies of accommodation so that they could infiltrate the structures. Rather they evangelized with vigor because they were absolutely convinced that every believer had equal access to Jesus, that each could be saved on personal confession of faith in Jesus, and that following Jesus in discipleship was the greatest human joy even though it may culminate in martyrdom. These understandings permeate the writings and testimonies of that era.

As generations pass and as traditions slowly take the place of spiritual renewal, the tendency is to place something else in the center of the Christian fellowships, be it a great idea like concern for humanity or some parochial view of the Bible or simply a need to keep the denomination going. This is why all of God's people must experience renewal continually, or at least in each generation, so that commitments other than to Jesus can be relegated to their secondary or tertiary position. Menno Simons kept repeating 1 Corinthians 3:11: "For no other foundation can anyone lay than that which is laid, which is Jesus Christ."

The believers' church produced community or fellowship. This was the proof of the emergence of a new creation. It was powerful and it shook Europe. Here was a group of adult believers who voluntarily bound themselves into discipling fellowships as equals with only a bare minimum of hierarchy. The fellowships were not peripheral in their theology, the church was an organic part of the very movement of the Spirit.

The denominations which resulted from this renewal, such as the Mennonites, have a high view of ecclesiology; they are convinced of the need for community. But they are not very sure about the nature of the church because they are ambivalent about the place of Jesus Christ in these fellowships. This is the basic weakness in our missiology. If we can recover the exhilarating reality of the living presence of Jesus Christ as the actual center of our life together, whether it be in the home, the fellowship, or the denomination, then the rationale and the means of mission will come clear.

This search for the meaning of community or church is at the center of our theologizing and this is the place to look for reasons for our apostasy and weakness and it likewise is the place to look for the way to renewal. As a denomination, we are blessed by having an international community of brothers and sisters who can help in this process of the recovery of the pneumatic fellowships which can and should astound the world. The following paragraphs bring together some of the recent Anabaptist-Mennonite thinking on this subject and how it affects missiology.

Modern Mennonite Missiology

Yamada Takashi, a Japanese Mennonite pastor, sees this theme as not only central in the Scriptures, but as the basic theological fact in the life and ministry of the church.

> The good news for man and his world is that God is working to bring about total harmony and integration in the whole creation through Jesus Christ. Man recovers his true personhood as he finds himself in this saving grace of God. Here is the basis for the world mission.[4]

Yamada chose a rather quaint English word to convey this transcendent Christian reality which expresses the present experience of the cosmic plan; he calls it conviviality, "life together." It is in fact a festive word with an element of joy. "Enjoying life together" may be an accurate definition. We do not simply endure one another for the sake of Christ but actually praise God for one another; we enjoy one another.

In order to further the coming together of all things in Christ, Yamada encourages the church to recover its own identity as people of God. He believes that:

> Anabaptists' "confronting attitude"—voluntarism in mission—is a powerful challenge to the worldly powers, and a self-denial of one's egocentric, authoritarian control of others. So according to Anabaptist understanding, this confronting attitude inevitably takes a "servanthood stance" which is actually the basis for the community of disciples in brotherly love toward one another, and for the free, voluntary association of believers under the lordship of Christ.[5]

One of the problems which puts constant pressure on the community is the use of power. Our age identifies power

---

4. Yamada Takashi, "Responsible Self-hood and Anabaptist Understandings" *Mennonite World Conference Consultation on World Mission*, Hesston, Kan., 1978, p. 1.

5. *Ibid.*, p. 12.

with money, management, education, and technology. For good or for ill the modern mission movement was hastened by modern Western expansionism. The Anabaptists of the sixteenth century lived in a completely different context. They developed a theology of confrontation because they did actually confront the temporal powers of their time. Not so in twentieth-century mission. Modern Western missions rode the crest of a temporal expansionist power, mainly European.

It is very difficult for us to extricate ourselves from these contexts. The fact that we Mennonites made our peace, to a large extent, with these powers, affected not only our methodology but at some points our theology of missions. We lost sight, to some extent, of the ultimate vision and settled too easily for a program of church extension and social services instead of the multiplication of convivial fellowships in Christ. I realize it is hard to divide these two concepts but there is a subtle difference. Church extension can revolve around self. I still feel a bit uneasy when talking about "church planting." I would rather envision our task as bringing together loving fellowships in Christ who live out their lives in a world both friendly and hostile.

A major agenda item for the entire church, but particularly for missions, is the deployment of power. Power can unite but it can, and usually does, divide. The San Juan Conference of July 1975, held under Mennonite World Conference auspices, highlighted this as a crucial issue. That conference encouraged Western mission agencies to utilize their power to bring things under Christ, not to separate people as is so often the case. In many respects our way of going about doing things belies our commitment to Christian conviviality in which confrontation and servanthood can, indeed must, coexist.

Other Mennonite mission theologians have added credence to the theme of the fellowship in Christ as the center of mission. Marlin Miller identifies the purpose of mission as the bringing about of peace. He sees this as a natural result of Jesus-enthused conviviality. "The gospel of peace," he asserts, "is both a message and a corporate existence."[6] "A renewed vision of the gospel of peace as an integral part of the good news of Jesus Christ would have far-reaching consequences for missionary thought and practice."[7]

> It would mean a theological reorientation with respect to central, traditional, doctrinal formulations which have not been foundationally shaped by the social dimensions of the good news. . . . It would mean the renewal of the church as a Messianic community whose basis for existence derives not from national, ethnic, or cultural givens, but from an ever new corporate identity in Christ.[8]

Wilbert Shenk stresses the "kingdom of God" image as the rallying point. He, however, strikes the same note. "Jesus introduced a new missionary vision of religious, cultural, and political transformation which led to the creation of a new people who were free to live by the will of God."[9]

Robert Ramseyer explains further,

> One of the most apparent distinctives of a church with the Anabaptist vision will be the quality of fellowship and mutual concern which it displays. Within the fellowship there will be nothing of the distinctions between groups which may be

---

6. Marlin Miller, "The Gospel of Peace," *Focus* V, No. 4, No. I, Elkhart, Ind., 1977, p. 5.

7 *Ibid*, p. 1.

8. *Ibid.*, p. 5.

9. Wilbert Shenk, "Where Are We in Mission Today?" *Mission Focus* Vol. 4, No. 4, Elkhart, Ind., p. 5.

found in the natural society from which its members have come.[10]

Reflecting on his own missionary career in light of New Testament theology, Mennonite missionary John Driver writes,

> Evangelism is not simply saving individuals from hell for heaven, nor inviting them to repentance and then leaving them to struggle alone to be faithful to their confession that Jesus is Lord. Evangelism is calling men and women to repentance and inviting them to become part of the community of God's people which participate even now and here on earth in the kingdom of God which will finally come in all its fullness.[11]

He, too, sees the presence of Christ as the pivotal fact in the Christian fellowship. "It is the presence of Jesus in his disciple community," he asserts, "which makes the gospel we proclaim eternally contemporary."[12] "Even though it may be costly, the true criterion for evaluating our evangelistic practices is the formation of disciple communities obedient to Jesus."[13]

J. D. Graber cut through the fog with statements like this:

> Christ's kingly rule is established already in the hearts of the true believers, and the drawing together of such a group of those reconciled unto God through faith in Christ form the body of Christ on earth. These are the first fruits, the heralding, looking forward to the consummation of the eternal kingdom at his coming again.[14]

---

10. Robert Ramseyer, "The Anabaptist Vision and Our World Mission," *Mission Focus* Vol. 4, No. 4, Elkhart, Ind., p. 5.
11. John Driver, *Community and Commitment* (Scottdale, Pa.: Herald Press, 1976), p. 90.
12. *Ibid.*, p. 89.
13. *Ibid.*, p. 92.
14. Graber, pp. 11, 12.

The Anabaptist theology of mission will concentrate its attention—in fact, sees as the focus of its mission—the calling into being of visible, loving fellowships of believers, willed by God, redeemed, gathered, loved, informed, and gifted by Jesus Christ, and enthused by the blessed Holy Spirit.

Summary—Jesus in the Midst of His People

Additional Anabaptist sources would serve to reiterate the central New Testament thesis that God's plan is to bring all things together in Christ and that the church is where this is first happening on earth. I believe that we should courageously embrace this central truth as the starting point for our missiology as well as for our ecclesiology. Restated, it is that Jesus is actually present in all his fullness when persons who are redeemed by him live in loving fellowship. This does not mean that he is not present in the not-yet-believing world; to some extent he is there but his work is constantly hindered by the demonic machinations of evil powers. It is difficult for true peace to exist there because the creatures are still living in a state of rebellion. Where disciples meet, however, Jesus is actually there through the Holy Spirit's ministration to bring peace which has substance.

Toward Cosmic Reconciliation

Cosmic reconciliation begins when people who were formerly enemies forgive one another through Christ in fellowship. The living, energizing presence of Jesus Christ is not ethereal. He is alive in the fellowships. Our theology is not only Christological, it is Christocentric. We do, in fact, experience the presence of Jesus Christ in our life together. Using the imagery of Christ as the head and the fellowship as the body, we are brought up short. Our tendency to relegate Christ to a position of lofty "otherness" is not dealing honestly with the facts. Jesus is in the heavenlies, but he is also in the earthlies. We experience him in our fellowships. "Where two or three are gathered together in my name," he asserted, "there am I in the midst" (Matthew 18:20). The writer to the Hebrews uses a lovely word picture to explain it; "In the midst of the congregation I [Jesus Christ] will praise thee" (Hebrews 2:12).

Jesus Christ is the vision. The fellowship participates in that vision. The fellowship is where Jesus is in his ministry to his world. Mission theology is no less than that. It assumes that the fellowship, with Jesus in the midst, partakes of Jesus' total life—his forgiveness, redemption, ethics, love, and all the other graces. The fellowship is not only taught by Christ, but exhibits the totality of Jesus' life. The fellowships ask, "Are we doing at this moment of time what Jesus Christ, who is with us, wants us to do?"

It is enough that Jesus is among his people. In fact, his presence among his disciples is the sign of the beginning of the new age which leads incontestably to the omega point in history when all things will be reunited in Christ.

When we speak of the ultimate unification of all things in Christ, we are not talking about some kind of universalism now newly dressed which insists that all will be saved even if they do not want to be. But we do believe that some day every tongue will acknowledge that Jesus Christ is none other than who he said he is. Some will acknowledge out of joyful obedience, others will acknowledge out of rebellion, but all will acknowledge. To acknowledge and to obey, however, are two different things.

Grace and Law

Judgment is an essential aspect of Christocentric theology. Disobedience to Jesus Christ leads to all manner of dislocation, disharmony, and finally, destruction. In a sense the disobedient pronounce judgment upon themselves because they reject the only Savior who is none other than the center of all life. He is life itself. Outside him there is no life, only dislocation and death. No matter how disobedient creatures organize themselves, their organizations are doomed because eternal life is in Jesus, the Son, and in no one else. All other deities are by their very nature self-destructive because they have no life-giving power. But some disobedient spirits and persons will persist in their rebellion right up to the end. They shall be cast into outer darkness.

Having said this I would like to reiterate that Christians rejoice when shalom is experienced anywhere in the world and, in fact, they should be actively involved as peace-makers, even among unbelievers. It is better for people to live in peace with one another, to cooperate in unified commonwealth, than to kill one another. Christians take no satisfaction when they see alienation among God's creatures. In fact, they are pained by it. They do not simply shrug the shoulder and say, "That is all you can expect from such people." They try to do something about it even though they realize that a cessation of hostility which leaves God out of the picture is probably temporary. Christians should be about their Father's business which is to bring all things together in Christ. Our eschatological hope is expressed in our life together as believers around Jesus and it is also expressed in our involvement in the not-yet-believing community.

Peace and Christian Fellowship

We should, for example, not be complacent about the frightening build-up of nuclear weapons because we can rationalize that, after all, these are evil people doing evil things and they cannot stop their evil ways. Weapons of mass destruction are as loathesome to Christians as to anyone else, if not more so. Likewise we should not acquiesce when we see a privileged minority anywhere impose its will by coercion over what it considers lesser people for the purposes of exploitation. The followers of Jesus must show a more excellent way, the way of divine love. The Christians' desire for peace does not arise from some utopian idealism but is centered in the life of Jesus Christ who expresses through his body his longing that all creatures might live in peace. The church is enthused with an eschatological hope which it perists in sharing with dislocated, alienated creatures.

It seems to me that the image of Jesus Christ in the midst of his people provides for a resolution for our paradoxes. It is imagery which describes a reality. It assumes that Christians are in the world but are not fashioned by the world. Being both "in" but "not of" are the outworking of the gracious presence of Jesus Christ. All paradox is resolved in Jesus. If we can actually give ourselves to living with one another in Christian love as Jesus Christ takes up residence in our midst, we will not be concerned about guaranteeing equal time to being "in" the world on the one hand and being "not of" the world on the other. We are involved in this world and yet separated from it. We shall be actively at work playing our part by grace in the ultimate drama of bringing everything together under Jesus Christ and for that we must be both "in" but not "of" the world.

The Key to Following Jesus, Spiritual Renewal

What, therefore, is required for a new vision for the mission of God on the earth? It is indeed nothing less than a new vision, a new appreciation, yes, a new experience of Jesus Christ of Nazareth.

And how is this to happen? I believe through a revitalization of our own lives and the life of our fellowships by participating in a living relationship with our living Savior and Lord. The center of our existence is not a new resolution, a new concern for humankind, a new idea; nor is it tribal memory or some blessed legend about a great teacher of ages gone; the center of our existence is the Christ who wishes to be active through us in bringing all things into subjection to the Father.

This requires that we take our common worship more seriously because in worship we acknowledge that we submit our wills to the will of him who stands among us in power. And as we worship we take another step forward in the unification of all things. We also realize that it is the will of God that all people everywhere participate in Jesus-centered fellowship. And we are also made aware of the fact that the body, the fellowship, is the place on earth where this fact is announced and implemented.

It is really quite impossible to imbibe the Spirit of Jesus and then remain inactive in this world. Worship of God in Christ by the Spirit does not isolate us from our world; rather it directs us as to what our place is in this world which is, after all, God's world.

Sin Must Be Acknowledged

As we cluster around Jesus, we discover that we are sometimes rebellious creatures, even after we are convinced that we believe in Jesus and love him dearly. We look at ourselves through him and we discover sin in our lives. We are amazed that he is still with us. Through the ministry of the Holy Spirit, we bring our sins to him in humble confession and he forgives us among the brethren. He cleanses us with his poured-out life. Our cleansing enables us to walk transparently with one another. We are refreshed. Ongoing repentance is the only way to experience a vital relationship with Jesus Christ; otherwise, we are so quick to turn to our own ways. So the key to our walk with Jesus is repentance. Who would have thought that the way to revival is also the way to mission? It is the way of the broken heart taking its place in repentant faith before Jesus. It is the way of the re-joicing heart which sings of Jesus' worthiness. It is the way of the serving heart which washes the feet of this world in the basin of hope.

Mission Is Listening to Jesus

In Jesus Christ we are not of this world. Our heart resides in the heavenlies. But in Jesus Christ we are in this world to live in unity with his people and to so live in the world that all people will see what direction creation is moving. In Jesus Christ we have the freedom of lambs to frolic in the meadows; in him we also have the security of sheep in a stronghold. He is our good shepherd and we are his sheep. We come out and we go in as his voice leads. His sheep know his voice and they will not heed the voice of a hireling.

The mission imperative is upon us as much as it was on any generation. May we be so in tune with his voice that we will startle this world and in doing so startle the powers of evil, heralding a new age which is already visible, dim though that may be, in the fellowships of believers where Jesus has taken up his residence on earth.

"You will be my witnesses" Jesus prophesied, "to the end of the earth." And so we are and so we shall be forever.

Implications for Mission

1. Mission methodology conforms to Jesus Christ.

All methods employed by fellowships, institutions, and agencies should be consistent with the spirit of Christ. Methods contrary to the person of Jesus may not be used on the pretext that something is being done "for" him, as though he were far away. Ethics is the mind of Christ expressed through the brotherhood. Christ is the norm for ethical behavior in evangelism and service both in regard to the ends we seek to accomplish and the means of achieving those ends.

2. Mission agencies are also fellowships.

The center of mission is the local fellowship. But the local fellowships may mandate mission boards to plan for and give leadership to forms of mission which a particular local fellowship cannot do by itself. Mission board members also become a fellowship who meet in the name of Christ for mission. They serve under the mandate of the local fellowships and must never act contrary to the confidence placed in them. Similarly the staff members of mission agencies have received their mandate through commissioning by the board and also serve as a fellowship in Christ.

3. Church growth includes evangelism and nurture.

The integrity of the fellowship in Christ must be affirmed even though for various reasons the fellowship lacks maturity. Numerical growth must always be in tension with nurture. We recognize the mandate for evangelism, but evangelism should not be seen apart from the ongoing process of growth toward spiritual maturity and discipleship. The ministry of the church includes both evangelism and discipleship. As the fellowship grows with Christ in its midst, there is a growing conformity to Christ, as well as outreach in evangelism.

4. Fellowships share resources.

We recognize that Christian believers around the world represent a wide spread of economic levels. The Scriptures instruct us to share with generosity and creativity both our wealth and ourselves in ministries of compassion.

5. *Missionaries enjoy fellowship at home and abroad.*

The missionary is sent forth by the local congregation. That is his or her primary fellowship base. Although the missionary becomes part of the fellowship in the place to which he or she has been sent, he or she is always a missioner sent forth by the home fellowship.

Missionaries must participate in fellowships to experience the fullness of the blessing of Christ. It is not appropriate for them to live as self-contained individuals separated from the context of the local church in which they serve. The fellowship where they are is the way of the gospel and a sign of the coming unity in Christ.

FOR FURTHER READING

Graber, J. D. *The Church Apostolic*. Scottdale, Pa.: Herald Press, 1960.

Newbigin, Lesslie. *The Open Secret*. Grand Rapids: Wm. B. Eerdmans, 1978.

Schlabach, Theron F. *Gospel Versus Gospel*. Scottdale, Pa.: Herald Press, 1980.

THE AUTHOR

Donald R. Jacobs brings to his writing a lifetime of experience in missions. Together with his wife, Anna Ruth (Charles), and four children, he served as a Mennonite missionary in Tanzania and Kenya from 1953 to 1973. Following that, Don was director of overseas ministries of the Eastern Mennonite Board of Missions and also executive director of Mennonite Christian Leadership Foundation, both located near Lancaster, Pennsylvania.

Jacobs was born and reared near Johnstown Pennsylvania. He holds a PhD in religious education from New York University with a major in cultural anthropology.

While in Tanzania he served as bishop of the rapidly growing Mennonite Church there. He founded Mennonite Theological College in Musoma, Tanzania, and was instrumental in the establishment of the department of religious studies at the University of Nairobi in Kenya.

Jacobs travels abroad extensively as a consultant and lecturer in theological education and leadership training.